MYSTERIES

MYSTERIES

RITA ROGERS' FIRST-HAND ACCOUNTS OF THE AMAZING WORLD OF THE UNEXPLAINED

RITA ROGERS

PAN BOOKS

First published 2001 by Pan Books
an imprint of Pan Macmillan Ltd
Pan Macmillan, 20 New Wharf Road, London N1 9RR
Basingstoke and Oxford
Associated companies throughout the world
www.panmacmillan.com

ISBN 0 330 39079 1

5 7 9 8 6 4

A CIP catalogue record for this book is available from
the British Library.

Printed and bound in Great Britain by
Mackays of Chatham plc, Chatham, Kent

For Mo

Rita Rogers is a medium of Romany origin whose popularity and outreach has exploded not only since her first book was published, the bestselling *Reaching For the Children*, but as her reputation and the respect in which her work is held has grown. Rita can be reached by writing to her at Mill Lane Farm, Mill Lane, Grassmoor, Chesterfield, S42 5AD. She promises to read every letter she receives but can only reply if a stamped, self-addressed envelope is enclosed.

All the stories included in this book are true. Where permission for stories to be reprinted could not be sought, the names of people have been changed in order to respect privacy.

Acknowledgements

Rita Rogers would like to thank all those who have contributed to this book and also Robert Kirby, Gordon Wise and Jackie Highe.

Contents

MYSTERIES

Introduction by Natasha Garnett

Rita Rogers is today one of the best known, most respected and popular mediums – not just in this country, but in the world. Born in Nottinghamshire in 1941 and of Romany lineage, Rita was the second daughter in a family of six children and was raised in the mining town of Mansfield. She discovered that she had the 'gift' when she was only four years old and believes that she inherited it, along with a four-hundred-year-old crystal ball, from her grandmother Mary Alice Thompson, who was a Romany seer. As a young child, Rita was always hearing and seeing things – people, colours, images that she did not understand. These experiences terrified her and during her childhood this so-called 'gift' seemed to cause her more problems than it solved. Her mother, who was not a Romany, would often chastise her for 'romancin'', 'It was a word I heard so often during those years I came to believe it myself,' she says.

Try as she might to avoid her calling, the voices and visions Rita experienced would not leave her. She tried her best to suppress them but they continued to haunt her throughout her teenage years. It was not until she was in her twenties that she came to understand what they meant. Having tried and failed to live a normal, ordinary life as a housewife, hospital worker and mother to her four daughters she realized that she could no longer escape her destiny. In time, she became aware that her psychic powers were not something to be frightened of, but that they could be used to help people. She spent the next years practising on friends and local people before she turned 'professional'.

Rita's reputation has grown on a word-of-mouth basis. She doesn't advertise, she has no need to, which is perhaps a testimony to her very genuine gift. Every day she receives hundreds of letters and calls from all over the world asking for help and requesting readings. Her waiting list is now longer than ever, and she finds it almost impossible to take on new clients, reading mainly for people with whom she has a long-term relationship or for whom she reads in the course of her journalistic work.

She has written three (four including this) books on her work and writes weekly columns for *Bella* magazine, in the United Kingdom, and *New Idea*, in Australia. She has read for a number of high-profile clients to whom she has always remained discreet and loyal. In *From One World to Another* Rita talked about the nature of her relationship with the late Princess of Wales but has always vowed that she would never discuss the content of their readings. Rita has made numerous television and radio appearances both here and abroad, has been interviewed by Larry King on *Larry King Live* and has been the subject of two documentaries. And yet were you to meet this warm, wonderful, down-to-earth woman in person you would never realize any of this. 'Reading for a VIP or appearing on a television programme, means nothing to me,' she says. 'When you read for someone who has lost a child, suffered from an illness, or been so low that they have wanted to take their own life and you can in some small way help them, that's what matters. That's what makes me happy and convinces me that what I am doing is right.'

My first contact with Rita Rogers occurred in the summer of 1996. I had been commissioned by *Vogue* to write an article about mediums and had intended the piece to be a scathing, critical attack on the booming psychic industry and those who consulted psychics. To say that I was sceptical of psychics and mediums would be an understatement. No rational person could believe that it was possible to receive messages from 'beyond the grave', that their future could be determined by the shuffle of the pack of tarot cards, read through the glass of crystal balls or by any other means. Psychics to me were for people who had something missing from their lives, for people with nothing better to do with their time and money.

In the course of my research I visited over forty people who claimed to have psychic abilities, but I was not impressed. Most of them I spoke to or who gave me readings told me little more about myself than a stranger could. Some said I might travel, others alluded to the fact that I might have had a broken relationship in the past, that I may once have been unhappy and that I might have lost a grandparent. On the whole their bland generalizations did nothing to convert me to spiritualism.

The night before I was due to deliver my article, a colleague suggested I contact Rita at her home, in Derbyshire. I was told she was good, so good that her two-year waiting list boasted celebrity names. I was told she could give me a reading over the telephone because she was clair-audient, which means that she is able to hear voices in her head from the spirit world as well as being able to see things. And so, with some reluctance, I telephoned Rita and asked if she would read for me. To be honest I doubted that she would be able to tell me anything that would alter my views or would change the shape of my article. How wrong I was. Two hours later following my reading I was back at my computer rewriting my piece. That night, through the accuracy of this reading, Rita Rogers challenged everything I held to be true. A complete stranger had come up with details about my life – past, present and future that were so accurate and often so personal which no one, not even members of my family, could have possibly known. In one reading, Rita Rogers convinced me that she was genuine and changed the way I looked at things for ever.

Anyone who has ever come in to contact with Rita Rogers will tell you what a remarkable woman she is, not least for her extraordinary and genuine gift but because of the compassion and sympathy she freely gives to all who come into her life. Sadly, Rita cannot read for everyone who writes to or calls her, she simply just doesn't have the time or the energy. This is one of the reasons she set about writing her books – so that she could bring answers, comfort and hope to thousands of people around the world.

1. *The Sixth Sense*

We tend to believe only in what we see and know. In this age of science and reason we think that unless we have tangible evidence, that something exists, then in our view it doesn't. Unless we can see something, or hear it, touch it, smell or taste it, we doubt its existence.

Most of us are lucky enough to have five senses – touch, smell, taste, sound and vision – which we depend on to get through our lives. By utilizing them our lives become easier and more enjoyable. Our senses make this world a better place – we can see the beauty of the day, hear the birds sing and people talk. We can taste our food, smell the flowers, touch our loved ones and feel the rain upon our cheeks. We use our senses to guide us and keep us out of harm's way. We know when we are in trouble because we can see danger. We know when someone needs help because we can hear them crying, and so forth. To be blessed with all five of our senses is a truly wonderful thing.

I am one of the fortunate because I have all five of my senses and this has helped me in my life. I know what it is like to hear music or to see a beautiful view. I am able to taste delicious foods. I can smell the morning dew in my garden and feel the softness of a young child's skin. I am also blessed in another way because I have another sense – a sixth sense.

The majority of people are spiritually deaf and blind, and my 'gift', if you can call it that, is that I am able to see, hear and communicate with spirits. This sensitivity gives the ability to register vibrations, radiations and frequencies that cannot be captured by the five senses. I can tune into activity that to most of you is inaudible and invisible.

I inherited my sixth sense from my Romany grandmother Mary Alice Thompson. She was a well-known seer from Nottinghamshire and a proper gypsy. She spent her youth travelling all over the north of England selling fortunes and flowers to people she came across on her journey. I was close to my grandmother and loved to spend time with her as a child. She often said that I was gifted and had a sixth sense. As a child I was always hearing and seeing things, although I did not understand much of it. My mother, who disapproved of my grandmother and was embarrassed by our Romany heritage, would chastise me as a little girl when I told her what I had seen and heard. She would tell me to stop 'romancin'' or telling fibs. But my grandmother encouraged my gift. 'You'll see, Rette,' she used to say to me as I sat on her knee. 'One day you'll come to learn to use this gift of yours. You'll not be frightened of it and you'll realize that it can help people. You'll become famous for your gift and you will change a great many lives for the better.'

For many years I tried to fight my gift. As a teenager I wanted to fit in with the others and so cared little for this sixth sense, instead preferring to dance and to enjoy the attentions of the young men in our town. I married young, as my grandmother predicted, and my husband was not keen on me developing my psychic skills. Over the years I channelled my energy into other things – working in a hospital, as a grocer, as a landlady in a guesthouse and most of all motherhood. It was not until I was much older that I realized that I could no longer ignore this gift of mine and so I learnt to use it.

People often tell me that I am lucky to possess the skills I have. They like the idea of being able to talk to their friends and relations in the spirit world, and finding out first hand what their future holds. They think it would be fun. Mediumship is not just a bit of fun. I'm not here to sit and sell fortunes like ice creams at the end of the pier. Mediumship is hard work. It's not something that you can learn – you have to be born with this gift and it can be a burden. For all its rewards I often wish that I was leading an ordinary life. Reading for people can be very draining and difficult. You see so much suffering and torment, so much pain and hurt. And at the end of the day it's hard to walk away from that and get on with your own life. You can't turn mediumship on and off to suit you. The gift is with you twenty-four hours a day, seven days a week. This is not an occupation but a vocation. (I always find it strange filling in forms and writing the word 'medium' in the job description box, so I usually just put consultant.) If I get a call in the middle of the night from someone who is distraught then I know that I have to take it – because my job is to help others. That is why I was given this gift by the spirit world in the first place.

But that said, my grandmother was right when she predicted that one day I would realize how much good this gift could do, how much happiness and hope I could give to others by learning to master my sixth sense. You only have to see a person's face after you have made contact and communicated with their loved one in spirit to know that what you do is rewarding and worth-while. When I can sit with a mother and tell her that I really do have her child in spirit and that they are warm, happy and well, and I am able to prove this to her, then I realize that this sixth sense is indeed a gift.

HOW MEDIUMS WORK

As a medium I act as a channel from one world to another. I am in a way nothing more than an amplifier who is able to hear messages from the spirit world and pass them on to the person here on earth.

Mediumship is about sensitivity and comes into being when my gift or sixth sense is used in close co-operation with spirit guides. Each medium has a special spirit guide appointed to them by the spirit world. The spirit guide helps the mediums to fine-tune their skills and senses, and also is my first port of call when I begin a reading. My spirit guide is a North American Indian called Running Water. When I need to read for someone I always ask him to come forward to me and bring the spirits through to me.

A medium's sixth sense can be divided into two different sensory perceptions – clairvoyance and clairaudience. Not all mediums have both of these senses, but if they do, they work with the sense that is strongest to them. Clairvoyance, which literally translates as clear vision, is the ability to see images and symbols passed on to the medium from the spirit world. Clairaudience, which means clear hearing, is the ability to hear the messages from the spirit world. I receive a lot of clairvoyant images but the majority of messages I get are clairaudient.

When mediums hear or see spirits they are not actually utilizing their physical eyes or ears. Instead they are using their inner eye or inner ear. The messages I get come through my solar plexus and the sensation is like having a voice within my head. It is distinct from anything you would normally hear. The voice, the sound, comes from within rather than something you hear outside.

The reason I am able to conduct the majority of my readings on the telephone is because I am clairaudient. I hear messages that are only audible to me and I am able to relate that message to the person I am reading for, or the recipient. It is similar I suppose to a conference call, and my role is to act as an amplifier to pass these messages on.

The reception of a spirit message can vary a lot. The message can come through extremely clear or it can be faint and barely audible. Sometimes it depends on how close you were to the person who is talking to me in spirit – if the bond was very strong between you, the messages I get come through strongly and quickly. If you do not know anyone well in spirit the contact I make with the spirit world might take a little longer. There are other factors that also affect the strength of the communication I have. A reading may not go well because I am distracted by outside noises, which means that I am not able to fully focus my mind on the reading, or it can be that I am not on form that day. Readings require the utmost concentration so anything from stress to a headache can affect my readings. In these situations I would postpone a reading until I was feeling better.

One of the pitfalls of having this sixth sense is that I hear messages throughout the day. A trip to the supermarket or a quick evening meal in the local pub can be a terrible trial. I can be standing at the checkout when I'll get the shop assistant's grandmother asking me to warn her of something! Or I can be in the pub when I get an image in my head of a red van and have to ask the landlord whether he should get his brakes checked. It is not only disruptive to my life but also quite embarrassing having to approach people. Often when the voice comes to me I think to myself, 'Oh no, here we go again.'

When I am doing my real readings I like to be in the right environment. To be able to hear messages from the spirit world I have to be somewhere private, quiet and without distraction. This is why I created my reading room, where people are shown when they come to me for a reading or where I will sit when I conduct a reading over the telephone.

Contrary to what you might be thinking this room isn't dark, draped and with a large round table with a crystal ball as a centrepiece. Instead it is a light and airy sitting room with a beautiful view of the valley below, which I find very calming. There are no 'props' here. I don't have a pyramid, I don't believe in tarot cards and although I inherited a 400-year-old crystal ball from my Romany grandmother, which my mother had for a time, I never use it. What you *will* find in my room, however, is a copy of the family Bible, which I keep by my chair, and a crucifix from Jerusalem. I keep these because I am a Christian and believe very much in God. This surprises some people, but like other Christians I believe that when we die we live on – that there is an afterlife and that there is a heaven.

I like to do all my readings from my reading room because it is private and peaceful. I get many requests from television companies to 'read' for audiences or from organizations asking me to do platform readings but I am very uncomfortable with this. As a rule I don't like to read in front of large crowds because readings are very personal experiences and should, I think, always be conducted in private. I am not here to perform for people but to help them.

The messages I receive are often deeply personal and private and the whole experience can be incredibly emotional for the person I am reading. When a spirit makes contact with me it is usually because they have something intimate to relate to the recipient. It may be something that you do not want to share with a group of strangers. If a spirit comes through and makes contact with me it is because they want to communicate with you properly. They don't come forward purely to entertain others or to make me look genuine. I find that spirits don't respond well in large gatherings, and anyway, put yourself as a medium in a room filled with 500 people and you'll get a thousand spirits all wanting to talk at once, so this is something that I try to avoid. So I created my reading room as an intimate and peaceful surrounding not only for myself but also for the spirits. This is a room where they know that they are safe and welcome.

The process of a reading is quite formulaic. When a person calls or visits me for a reading I will make sure that I am ready and relaxed before I begin. If it is their first reading I take a little time just chatting to them before I begin to read. I do this not to find out anything about them – in fact these conversations usually revolve around the weather and other neutral subjects – but to put them at their ease. Contacting the spirit world and visiting a medium can be a harrowing experience. Most people that come to me for the first time are extremely nervous not just of me and the process but also I think because they are worried that they might not be able to make contact with their loved one at all.

The next thing is to ask the person I am reading for what their star sign is. I do this not to get a profile on them or to second-guess their lives but simply because I like to get an idea of their personality. I never like to keep a message from people no matter how bad it is – if a spirit tells me something it is because they want it to be relayed – but I prefer to know how to pass that message on. I may tread more carefully if I know that someone is more sensitive than others. You can be more straight-forward and matter of fact with a fire sign, for example, than you can with water signs, who on the whole are much more sensitive.

I ask the recipient to try and remain as quiet as possible once the reading begins. The reason for this is not only because I need to concentrate 100 per cent on what the spirit is saying to me but also because I am only human. This way I avoid being prejudiced or influenced by what the recipient tells me and I avoid auto-suggestion. If someone starts telling me about his or her life then it is hard to ignore that information. The only thing I do ask people at the beginning of the reading is whether they know anyone who has passed over into the spirit world in the last five years. This question is essentially rhetorical. I am not actually asking for an answer – what I am doing is asking them to focus their minds on the person thus encouraging the spirit to come forward.

When contact is made with the spirit the reading begins. I find that spirits always begin their communication with me in the same way – they tell me who they are. They may give me their name or initial, or tell me what their relationship with you is. If they simply give me an initial I find that as the reading progresses they usually give me their Christian name.

The next step is to tell me how they passed over. Spirits do this not only to convince you that you are talking to them but also to let you know that however painful or horrific their death was, they are now fine. They will say to me, for example, that they suffered from cancer but they are now without pain, or that they died in a car accident but their soul survived the crash. The spirits will then name other people who you know are in spirit to show you that they are not alone.

Spirits want us to believe that we are communicating and speaking to them so they will come out with information which perhaps you were not expecting. This may seem trivial to some but they will tell me, for example, what their nickname was, what your family dog is called, or mention the place or occasion when you last saw each other. They are giving you positive proof that they are around and also that I am not making it up. Often these messages, you see, mean absolutely nothing to me, but these obscure specific details are what it takes to make you believe that they are still alive, albeit in another place.

During the reading my voice doesn't change or alter but people do tell me that I tend to adopt the characteristics of speech that the spirit had in life. When I hear the spirit they will talk in the same manner to me as they did here in life. They may be extremely chatty, or softly spoken, they may like to have a joke or even be quite bossy. During a good reading all these characteristics and idiosyncrasies should come through.

Transfiguration or materialization is the means by which a spirit shows itself via a medium to those on the earth plane. This is one of the rarest of all psychic phenomena. There are a great many mediums who have both clairvoyant and clairaudient skills, but very few mediums have enough of a gift to be able to make a spirit materialize.

In a transfiguration the spirit entity forms a duplicate of its image, or a projection, and manifests that image on to or nearby the medium. As in clairaudience and clairvoyance the medium acts as a channel through which the spirit can appear, and then as a screen or a canvas on to which the spirit can project itself.

Unlike an apparition, the spirit shows itself only because it has been asked to do so at the request of the medium. The medium must have first of all made contact with the spirit and been in communication with them. The medium then asks the spirit to come forward and to try and show themselves. She or he will enter a trance, concentrating on the spirit, and with any luck the spirit will come forward and transpose its image on to the face of the medium or nearby where the medium is sitting or standing.

What you are seeing is not the actual person who has passed over but an image of them. If you reached out and touched them you would feel nothing and they cannot come to you and touch you. The transfiguration involves the use of ectoplasm, which is almost invisible. It is a colourless, slightly fluid and cloudy substance similar to steam or a morning mist. This substance moves into a structure and forms the image of the spirit.

Transfiguration is rare and difficult to do, not least because it puts such a physical strain on the medium. If the medium is not fully focused on the spirit or distracted in any way the transfiguration will not occur. The trance needed to summon the spirit can be so intense that the medium is often unaware of what has happened until a few minutes after the spirit has shown itself. To allow the spirit to come it is very important that the medium goes into this trance and empties their mind. For the medium it is like entering a very deep sleep. Upon waking I feel dazed and confused, and usually I find I am left with the most terrible pounding headache.

Before the medium enters the trance they will ask the spirit to come forward, and most importantly remind the spirit that after it has shown itself it must not take possession of the medium's body but return to the spirit world. Then I will momentarily close my eyes or fix them on the person I am reading for so that I am able to focus my mind. I empty my head of all thoughts and begin slowly to go into a trance-like state. It is rather like meditating. At this point my vision will go hazy and start to blur and I will not see or hear anything until the spirit has left me and I come out of the trance.

What the recipient sees next can vary. Some materializations are quick and the person I am reading for may only get a glimpse of their spirit. In other cases they can last for what seems to them like ages – although probably it is just a matter of minutes – and the image can be very clear. Either way the process never changes. I always ask the recipient to focus on my eyes. Once this eye contact is established they will notice that very gradually a mist seems to form around my face and body. Within a minute or two this mist will have formed all around me so that all they can see in the now darkened room are my eyes. Bit by bit the mist will start to clear and begin to reform into an image of the spirit. Features will begin to take shape around the face and shoulders. It is a slow process so you have to be patient. People tell me that the mouth and nose are usually the first features to take shape. In some cases this may be all that can be seen but in other transfigurations it is possible for the image to be strong and vivid and recognizable

Witnessing a materialization is an emotional and intense experience, and not one that I would recommend to everyone that comes to me for a reading. There is a great difference between wanting to hear from your loved one in spirit and seeing them. For a transfiguration to work the bond between the recipient and the spirit must be extremely strong, and the spirit must really want and feel a need to show itself.

I am very selective about who I do these materializations for. This is not a performance or some kind of psychic party trick that I put on for the amusement of others. It is a very intimate moment between you and your loved one.

Of course there are many different ways of reading people. To look at someone's past, present or future you don't have to make direct communication with the spirit world. It is possible, for example, to read a person simply by looking at them. You can tell a lot about someone by looking at what we call their 'aura'. An aura is a luminous coloured substance that surrounds the body. The aura isn't visible to everyone's eyes. You need to be trained to look for an aura – but you don't have to be a medium to see one. The colour and the width of their aura can establish a person's welfare. The colours of the aura denote character, emotional and spiritual well-being. Red, for example, denotes anger, yellow is for wisdom and grey is for fear. People who are spiritual tend to have golden auras.

Then there is the palm. Your palm is an intrinsic part of you and the lines on your hand that were formed within your mother's womb reflect your destiny. You can measure your life span on your palm and see how many marriages and children you will have. It's your life's map. It tells you where you are going and where you have been – but it cannot give you specifics.

The crystal ball tells you the journey that you will make in life. The small stars of light reflected within the ball are read when the ball is placed in your hand. By examining the way the light and you interact with the stars the reader can tell you your destiny.

Psychometry is practised by mediums when they want to find out more about the person they are reading for or the person they are trying to contact. Here you take something that belongs to the person, something personal, such as jewellery, and hold it. By feeling the vibrations of this object it is possible to pick up information about the person who owns it. Psychometry can be useful in cases where a medium is trying to find a missing person. Although I can read auras and palms, practise psychometry and own a crystal ball, I don't tend to use them in my work, only because I don't find them nearly as reliable or as enlightening as communicating with spirits directly.

There are two forms of mystical and supernatural practices to which I am vehemently opposed – tarot cards and the ouija board. The reason I am against the use of fortune-telling cards is that I really don't see how you can read a person's destiny by simply shuffling a deck of cards. Should you have your cards read twice, the likelihood of laying out the same sequence of cards more than once is extremely slim. You do not have two destinies; you do not have two lives. Unlike your palm, your aura, your piece of jewellery, your spirits, these cards don't belong to you – so I really don't see how they can help us interpret or read our lives.

My opposition to the use of ouija boards doesn't stem from the fact that they don't work. My problem with them is that they do! But I would not advise anyone who is interested in spiritualism or contacting their loved ones to have anything to do with them. Spirits contacted via the ouija board don't come from the spirit world but are spirits that have not yet ascended. They don't come with peace or love or to guide you, they come to make trouble. The repercussions of meddling in the ouija board are serious, as we shall see in Chapter Five. Our spirits only come to us when they know it is safe, and they don't go near ouija boards, so my advice to anyone wanting to communicate with their loved ones on the other side is to try and find a reputable medium.

The main motivation for writing my books is that sadly I cannot give everyone who calls or writes an appointment. I must get more than a hundred letters a day now from around the world asking and begging me for a reading. It breaks my heart to receive them because I know that I cannot see them all. I already have a two-year waiting list for people and as a rule I try now to do only ten readings a week. I have had to cut down simply because I am not getting any younger and I need more time to myself. A reading is draining on the mind and body, and following a year of ill health I decided to slow down a bit.

I have always found it hard selecting appointments. I will try and make appointments for those people who have lost children because this is my field and it is something close to my heart, but I find it hard even to make room for these.

One Friday evening I came home to find that my assistant had left for the weekend. It's my assistant's job to take my calls, make appointments and try to squeeze in all my appointments. My daughter Kerry usually does this for me but because she was away on holiday I had got Julie to stand in. Julie is incredibly efficient so when I got in that evening I found an A4 pad with a list of names for me to call. There must have been twenty or more messages from all over the world left on the answering machine from people asking for appointments. I groaned, 'You'll be lucky,' I thought. 'I'll probably be in my grave by the time I get round to seeing you.'

I was completely worn out as it was, and had no intention of calling any of them that night. I needed a hot bath, some time to relax and an early night. I was due to open a local fete the next morning and I was already beginning to regret having agreed to that. To be honest I hadn't been feeling on good form for ages, I was overtired, doing too much and I was getting run down. I needed some rest. The last thing I had in mind was to do another reading!

Sitting there slumped in my armchair in my reading room,

I suddenly felt the presence of a little boy. He had just walked through the door of my reading room and was looking for me. It was as though he was calling my name, then all of a sudden there he was – this tiny thing, with wispy hair, a little ferret face and enormous eyes! He stood in my reading room as though it was the most normal thing in the world. 'Hello,' he said to me, ever so politely. 'My name's Jack.'

'Hello, Jack! I'm Rita,' I said, sitting forward in my chair so that I could get a better look at him. I was wondering to myself whether I had read his parents before, if I had spoken to him in a reading, but nothing came to me. 'How did you pass over?' I asked him.

Jack shrugged in the way little boys do. 'I don't know, I just did,' he said, now looking at his feet.

'I want you to ring my Mummy,' he said quickly. 'And I want you to say that I am with my Nana Kathleen.'

'Oh, well of course I will Jack,' I said, wondering how on earth I was going to find his mummy. Jack told me he was from round here.

'Tell my Mummy I'm twiddling my Nana's hair now. Tell her that William, my brother, can have my train set. And that I have met Rebecca. Tell Mummy I'm warm too. Tell her I'm not cold,' he said.

At that moment little Jack disappeared, but I heard a voice in my head. It was Kathleen – she was telling me that she passed over with cancer and she was saying a name to me but I couldn't quite make it out because her voice was so faint. It was either Joy or Joyce. 'Please ring her and tell her he is with me,' she said to me. 'Please!'

And then, just like that, she went too and I was left sitting in the reading room wondering what on earth to do next. They hadn't told me who they were. I didn't know how I was going to be able to make contact with them; I didn't even have a surname, let alone a telephone number. I couldn't even be sure of the Christian name. I didn't know what to do. Then for some reason, and I don't know why I did it, I reached for the pad with the messages on it. I looked at the list and could not take my eyes off it. 'What am I doing?' I thought. 'I'm supposed to be resting.' I then found my finger instinctively going down the list – it was as though someone had taken hold of my wrist and was guiding my hand down the paper. It stopped right in the middle of the list on a telephone number. 01623 began the code. 'Mansfield,' I thought. 'Mansfield's in Nottinghamshire not in Derbyshire,' I thought to myself. And the name on the list wasn't Joy or Joyce – but Alan. I didn't know what I was doing but I picked up the telephone. Someone was willing me to make this call although I didn't know who. 'If there isn't a Joy or a Joyce there just pretend you've got the wrong number,' I reasoned to myself. 'That's ridiculous,' I thought. 'He rang you – just return the call.'

I dialled the number. It started to ring. A man answered the call. 'Hello?' he said.

'Hello, this is Rita Rogers,' I said. 'I'm just returning your call.'

There was a pause and then he said 'Oh thank God! You have answered my wife's prayers . . . I'm sorry, it's just I didn't expect to hear from you so quickly.'

'Is your wife a Joy or a Joyce?' I asked.

'She's a Joy,' he said, sounding quite taken aback.

'Have you recently lost a little boy called Jack?' I continued.

'Oh my goodness,' he said, overwhelmed, 'I think Joy had better hear this.'

Joy came to the phone and said to me, 'I have been praying and praying for my mum to bring Jack to you. When I couldn't get through to you on the telephone I asked her to bring him to you so that we could somehow get in touch.' Joy was now sobbing.

'Is your Mum Kathleen?' I asked her.

'Yes, she is!' she said.

'Your Mum brought Jack to me today, he says he twiddles *her* hair now and that you are not to worry about him because he is warm,' I explained.

'I asked her to find you!' Joy sobbed.

'Who is Rebecca?' I then asked her. I could hear a gasp at the other end of the phone.

'She was my baby girl,' she said. 'She died when she was only three months old.'

'And William?' I asked. 'Is William Jack's bother?'

'Yes!'

'Well Jack says he wants him to have his train set.'

'I can't tell you what this means to me. It means that I can get through the weekend. We don't bury him until Monday you see and I'm going to the Chapel of Rest tonight. I didn't even know if I was going to get through the night,' Joy said. She was crying uncontrollably now – but there was relief in her voice. The heavy sobs I had heard when she first came to the telephone had lifted.

That Sunday evening I rang Joy and Alan to wish them well for the funeral the next day. They thanked me for calling them. Joy said that after the call she ran from the house to her neighbours. She was crying hysterically but she was happy. 'He's OK,' she told them. 'And he's warm!' On Friday evening Alan and Joy had gone to the Chapel of Rest and kissed their boy goodbye. They thought before they spoke to me that this would be the hardest thing to do. Alan had been seriously concerned that Joy might not be able to survive the weekend. But after our conversation Joy understood. They kissed Jack and when they turned to leave Joy said to Alan, 'I can walk away, and I can sleep now, because I know that that's not Jack. I know he is safe now.'

Alan and Joy thanked me profusely for what I had done, which made me feel a little guilty! You see I hadn't done anything at all. It was all thanks to little Jack!

2. *The Greatest Mystery of All – Death*

Although death is life's greatest inevitability, it is also life's greatest mystery. From the moment we are born we are dying. Each day that we live brings us closer to the one unavoidable event of our lives. Death is inevitable. It is a fact of life. Yet despite this we live in constant fear of dying and death.

The reason for this is that we know so little about death. Our understanding of it is limited so we tend to fear it. We have little idea or evidence about what happens after we pass away, no knowledge of the other side, and we are frightened by the very idea of it. However bad this world has been to us, however painful or lonely our lives have been, most of us given the choice would rather stay here than enter the unknown.

I am not scared of death. Like my Romany grandmother, I look forward to the day that I'll leave this world and enter the next. Unlike most people, I perhaps have been given a better insight into what lies ahead, which has helped to ease my fears. My work as a medium has taught me that there is a life after this and it is a much better one. As Grandmother used to say, 'This is your hell, you'll not get worse than this.'

Different cultures, countries and religions have their own ideas of what the afterlife is like. Christians, for example, believe in a heaven for the good and a hell for the bad. Other religions such as Hinduism and Buddhism believe in a reincarnation back into this life. Spiritual cultures such as the North American Indians and the Aborigines believe that we leave our bodies to become spirits. It doesn't really matter what our interpretation of a life beyond this one is, but it is important that we can come to understand that there is one.

Even those who hold deep religious beliefs still tend to fear death. Whether or not we believe that the soul and spirit of a person survives beyond death, it is difficult to imagine in what capacity, for we have grown used to seeing things and thinking of experience in physical terms. We cannot imagine a life away from a physical world, one where we don't have an actual physical form.

As I always say death isn't a word I like to use. It is a cold and unattractive word that contradicts the reality. The experiences I have had in my own life and through my work have convinced me that after we *die* we live on, albeit in another form. I prefer to think of it as passing away, passing away from this world or, more accurately perhaps, a passing over to the next. I called my first book *From One World to Another* because this is exactly what happens when we die, pass away or pass over.

So death is not the end but the beginning of a different phase of eternal life, of a spirit life. The day on which we die is not the end of our lives but the beginning of the start of our new life. It is a second birthday. We leave this world behind and enter another one. We begin a new life, one that will last for eternity. In this chapter I want to look at what happens when we pass over and hopefully shed new light on the mystery of death.

WHAT HAPPENS WHEN WE DIE

I find that when people who have lost someone close to them come to me for a reading, their first question is always 'did they suffer?' As someone with spiritualist beliefs, and a medium who gets proof of an existence of an afterlife each and every day, I can usually reassure the people I am reading for that their loved one is now at peace. Sadly I cannot say that their loved one's death was painless. We all want our deaths to be painless and peaceful. Given the choice most of us would like to slip away in our sleep having reached a ripe old age.

I said earlier that I don't fear death. I don't because I know that there is a life after this. In many respects, given that it is a life without pain and suffering, I look forward to it. That said, I am only human, and like anyone else I fear pain and I fear *dying*. Anyone who knows me will vouch I am the world's worst traveller! I hate long car journeys, I am terrified of London taxis because they seem to drive so fast, but I think more than anything I hate aeroplanes. I have only been on one once and I hated it so much I cried throughout the whole journey. My fear stems from the fact that something might go wrong. I worry that the plane might crash and that is not how I want to die.

This may seem irrelevant, or even silly to those used to making long journeys, but I am trying to explain here that despite not fearing being dead or having passed over – I still mind about how I go. Like most people I would rather that it was quick and painless, and with any luck at home!

When someone we know passes over we want to think that

their last moments here on earth were happy. We would like to think that they didn't suffer. We hope that if their death was violent or sudden, as a result of an accident or foul play, that they were at least not conscious of what was happening to them. This is a perfectly natural reaction. We hate to think that their final moments were spent in pain or in fear.

I wish that for every reading I did I could sit down and say to the people left behind that their loved one passed peacefully. But I can't. However, what I can say to the widower who lost his wife to cancer, to the mother whose daughter was murdered, to the boyfriend whose girlfriend died in the crash and so on, is no matter how they suffered at the time of their death they are peaceful, well and happy now. I'm not in the business of offering platitudes. When I say this to people I am actually telling the truth. When we reach the spirit world, once we pass over, we are without suffering. We are at peace.

We tend to fear dying because we know so little about the actual process. Our fear of passing away originates from a terror of the unknown and our inability to imagine a life apart from this one. When we lose someone who has been close to us not only do we grieve their passing but we worry about the way that they went. Spirits are acutely aware of this: once they have passed over they are still with us, they visit us throughout the day and night, they see our grief, our torment and our anxieties. This is why, when I give a reading to someone who has lost a loved one, the spirit will first of all tell me how they passed over. They will describe what happened in their final moments here on earth and they will tell me how they are now. They do this not only to prove to you that you are communicating with them but also to show you that however bad their passing was they are now fine and they don't want you to worry.

From the communications I have had with the spirit world and from my own experiences, which I shall describe later on, the process of dying is as follows. Whether we are ill, in an accident or simply pass over with old age, once our body has shut down and stops functioning our spirit leaves our body. It has no need to be inside it any more. So from the moment that our 'life' ends the spirit has already begun its journey to the afterlife. The spirit moves away from the body and then is called towards the spirit world. At this point the spirit has lost all concept of pain or suffering. Any illness, pain or suffering is left with the body.

I find that one of the most common anxieties that the bereaved suffer from is wondering whether their loved one is cold. We hate to think of the person that we love lying cold in a hospital, in a mortuary, or in a coffin in the ground. When we do pass over the temperature of our dead body drops, because our metabolism has stopped functioning and our heart has stopped pumping blood around our bodies. It is important to remember that whilst the body of the person you have loved is cold, *they* are not cold because they have left that body, because it is obsolete and they have entered another world. So when I am asked this, the simple and truthful answer is no. The cold hand that you touch, the cold cheek that you kiss goodbye to, these no longer belong to them. The person that you love has gone. They went long before their body had a chance to get cold. The images that we associate with passing away such as darkness, cold, isolation and decay –these things are not happening to your loved one, they are happening to the body, the shell they occupied here on earth. Your loved one has already moved on.

As soon as we 'die' the spirit begins its journey towards the spirit world. I am not sure how long this process takes – but given the readings I have done for people whose loved ones have just passed over I don't think it takes that long. It could be a matter of hours or days. The spirit is 'collected' or 'fetched' by those they know who are already in spirit. This could be your parents, or your grandparents, for example, or perhaps another relative or friend. People who don't know anyone in the spirit world shouldn't worry that they won't be collected because we are all met by someone – it could be our guardian angel or an ancestor but whoever it is they still come with love and warmth. And so having been met by their loved ones and guardians the spirit is then accepted into the spirit world.

THE SPIRIT WORLD

I always find it difficult to describe the spirit world. It isn't a three-dimensional place. It has no geographical location. It is neither above us or below us. It just is. The spirit world is not made up of white clouds, nor is it a furnace of flames. The only way I can describe it is by likening it to a state of mind. I am not saying that it is a construct of our imaginations but that it is akin to a higher level of consciousness than any place we might have visited here on earth.

In many ways dying and entering the spirit world is very similar to what happens when we go to sleep at night and dream. During the night while we are sleeping and our physical bodies rest, our mind travels into another level of consciousness and we become free to travel to other worlds. During these dreams we look the same, people that we meet recognize us, we have adventures and travel, and are capable of emotion, but none of this appears to have any physical effect on our bodies. We have these experiences and yet we do so without the need of a physical form. The spirit world has no physical or fixed boundaries and when we leave this world we are not taken to another universe.

Spirits seem to be able to travel easily between both worlds. The messages that I receive in my readings prove this. It is, for example, normal for a spirit to refer to something that has happened on the earth plane since they have passed away. This could be a significant event like the arrival of a baby or it could be something trivial like the fact you have just redecorated a room in your house. The reason they give me this type of information is to let you know that although they have gone, they are still with us.

When we die we all go to the spirit world. I mention this only because I cannot tell you how many letters I get from people worried that they might not make it into spirit world, either because of their religious beliefs or lack of them, the fact that they have done something bad in life, or simply because they don't think that they have been good enough.

Recently I had a letter from a woman who said her mother was distraught because her son had died as a baby and she had never had a chance to get him christened. That was 60 years ago. This poor, elderly lady had lived with this burden of guilt and worry all those years, unable to tell a soul out of shame! She shouldn't have tortured herself like that because we all go to the spirit world no matter what our religion or beliefs. Even the most ardent atheist is welcomed into the spirit world.

Although the spirit world is not a geographical place it does have a structure. There seem to be seven different astral planes in the afterlife, with each plane reflecting the level of our spiritual being. The first plane is for those who have committed a terrible crime in this life without showing any sign of remorse. There is no hell in the spirit world. If you have badly sinned in this life this is where you will go in the next. Should we commit murder or rape or some other heinous crime, and we have not asked for forgiveness or redeemed ourselves here, we will do 'our time' as such on that plane. It is the lowest rung of the spiritual ladder and until we learn humility and show remorse we will remain there. Spirits on this plane are not free to travel either between planes or to the earth plane. So someone who has been evil here cannot come back to haunt you when they pass over.

The structure is graded on levels of spiritual purity and reflects the way we lived our lives. We gravitate when we die to the spiritual plane to which we are most suited. The better the person you have been in life, the higher the plane you ascend to. The seventh plane is for those who have reached a level of spiritual perfection. My understanding is that most adults enter the spirit world on the fourth plane. A child whose life has been cut short or a person who has suffered a great deal in this world, or has sacrificed a lot for others, may go straight to the sixth or seventh plane. The spiritual hierarchy, however, is not fixed. When we enter the spirit world the idea is that we grow and improve spiritually, and as we do so we move up the ladder until we eventually reach the seventh plane. Because in spirit we are constantly evolving and becoming better we can only move up this hierarchy. There is nothing we can do in spirit that could result in us being sent down a plane – simply because there are no sins to commit.

So as you see there is no heaven or hell as such in the spirit world. Whichever plane you ascend to, even if it's the first, you will find that this is a better place than anywhere you have been here, for in spirit there is no pain, no suffering, only love.

SPIRITS

When we die we discard our physical body because it is no longer of any use to us. It becomes obsolete. To survive this world we needed our body but when we move to the spirit world it is no longer necessary to our survival. In many ways the human body is nothing more than a vehicle we use to transport ourselves through life. Because our lives are so rooted in the material we tend to put a lot of emphasis on the importance of the physical form. We associate an individual with what they look like, how they are physically and so on, but this is not our identity. Our identity lies not in our organs but in our souls. Our souls make our characters the way they are. Although our physical forms can affect the way we are, they do not shape who we are. When we die our soul lives on, it is just our body that has died.

So when we die we don't *become* spirits because that spirit is already within us. Passing over is a continuation of life, albeit in another form, and when we enter the spirit world we are still the same person we were in this life. I always compare passing over to the metamorphosis of the caterpillar into the butterfly, with the process of dying being the chrysalis. From a land-bound creature we become a thing of great beauty, free to fly wherever we want.

In spirit we seem to replicate an image of the body we had in this life – only it does not suffer from disease, infirmity or handicap. As I have said before in my other books we are all perfect in spirit. Whatever physical, emotional or mental problems we suffered from here are taken away from us in spirit. Again this is not something I say to people just to make them feel better. In my readings I have seen this time and time again. I have read for a father whose daughter in this life had been blind. I didn't know this when the reading began but the first thing this girl told me to tell her father was that she could see now. I transfigured the spirit of a girl who suffered from Down's Syndrome only to have her mother break down in tears. 'What is it?' I said afterwards. 'Did it upset you terribly?'

'Oh no,' she replied. 'It's just she looked so beautiful, she was perfect in every way.'

I believe that people who have suffered terribly in this life either through illness or handicap should look forward to entering the spirit world because in the next life they will be free from the shackles of the human body. They should know that whatever affliction they suffered from in this life will be put right in the next. I read for a couple who were amazed that I could hear and receive messages from a relation because in this life he could not speak; he had suffered from cancer and had to have his voice box removed. Yet they knew I was talking to him because he was telling me things that no one could have possibly made up.

Another question that people always ask me is what do we

look like in the spirit world. Unlike the human body the spirit body is not a fixed form. We view it subjectively. When you pass over you will appear to your children as you did as their mother, to your husband as you did as his wife, to your grandchildren as you did as their grandmother. I believe this to be true because of my own experiences, either transfiguring spirits or having seen the spirits of people I knew in this life.

Just because someone has passed over does not mean that they are no longer with us. You must not think that because you have buried your loved one in the ground and said goodbye to them that they have left you for good. They haven't. Spirits are free to move from their world and ours and do so often. They do this because they love us, because they want to see us and they like to protect us.

I find in my work that even people who have strong beliefs in an afterlife are surprised by this. They believe that their loved one is in another and better place, which is of course true, but they may not realize that spirits are able to travel from that better place back here to earth to be with us and look after us. A lot of people who come to me for readings are surprised that I am able to tell them things about the present. They imagine that the spirit will want to reminisce or to hear news about what is happening now that they have gone. So they are often taken aback during their first reading when I come out with information about what is going on in the present! I may tell them that I know that they have recently redecorated, have moved jobs, have converted the loft, have bought a new car, dog, cooker and so on. 'How do you know that?' they ask. I know that because your spirit is aware of everything that is going on in your life. This kind of information may seem trivial to some people but I cannot stress the value and significance of it. Firstly, because specific intimate details like these prove that I am in actual communication with the spirit in question, and also because it means that I can show and prove that spirits are around you and spend time with you. They are there at all the important times in your lives. When you are down, when you are happy, they are there to see their grandchildren, or your daughter's school play. They come to that wedding, watch over you when you drive at night and they are there at their own funeral, they see the flowers, they see the tears. Just because you cannot see or hear your loved ones now they have entered the spirit world does not mean that they don't exist. They are with us throughout the day and night as the following story shows.

My hairdresser Helen used to visit a Mrs Romsey about twice a month to do her hair. She lived with her husband not far from here in Derbyshire. The couple were elderly and inseparable. One morning when Helen was round here giving me a trim I asked Helen who Rosemary was. She stopped what she was doing, put her scissors down and had a think. 'Rosemary . . . ?' she said, shaking her head. 'I don't know any Rosemaries.'

'Are you sure?' I asked.

'I'm positive,' she said.

'That's very strange. Someone is coming to me with the name Rosemary. There's an elderly woman, she's not well, she'll not be with us long,' I said.

I think by now Helen's quite used to my ways. 'I swear I don't know a Rosemary, Rita!' she said and she carried on cutting my hair. Later that day Helen turned up at Mrs Romsey's house for her regular appointment but a woman she didn't recognize came to the door. 'Mrs Romsey's not here,' she said. 'She's had a stroke and is at the hospital.'

'Oh dear,' said Helen. 'Send her my best.' As she drove out of the street she noticed for the first time the street name: Rosemary Drive. When Helen called again that week to see how Mrs Romsey was, she was told by her husband that she had passed away.

Some weeks later I said to Helen, 'That woman I mentioned, she's gone now. She's telling me she went with a stroke.' Helen looked at me. 'Rosemary isn't her name, she says, that's where she lived, her name is Muriel,' I said. Helen just stared at me. 'She wants you to tell her husband that she misses him and that she comes to see him every night,' I continued. 'She comes just before he goes to bed, and she's telling me to tell him that she knows that every night before he goes to bed he has a piece of cheese.' Helen looked at me in disbelief.

The next day Helen called on Mr Romsey to offer her condolences. They were chatting when Helen asked him if he would like to talk to me. He seemed keen so it was arranged for him to come for a reading later that week. When the reading began I brought up the cheese because Muriel kept going on about it. Mr Romsey went red. 'I do have cheese before bed,' he said. 'Muriel would never let me have it when she was around because she said it was bad for me. But now that she's gone, well, I reckoned it wouldn't matter,' he told me, blushing!

ANGELS

I have said that when we get to the spirit world we all embark on a journey towards spiritual perfection and purity, but there are some people who, I believe, have begun that journey during their lives here on earth. I am not saying that these people are without sin or are 'perfect' but that there is an inherent goodness in these people that makes them very special.

When we lose a loved one, particularly if their life has been cut short, we always end up asking the same question, 'why?' When a person has so much to live for, shows such promise and has brought so much joy and love into our lives it seems tragic that their life has been cut short. We cannot understand why they have been taken from us. We think fate cruel for depriving that person, and ourselves, of their life. Death, particularly a sudden death, seems wrong and pointless, and we are often left wondering whether there is a god at all. For if there is a god then why would he take such a special person away from us? Why would he punish them in that way?

The loss of a young person is always hard to cope with, especially if you are a parent. I say this is the hardest of all griefs because the loss of a child threatens the natural order of things. As parents we believe that we will go first. Our children are supposed to outlive us and so burying your child, whatever their age, is an extremely difficult thing to do. In the cases I have seen where a parent loses a child it is hard for them to reconcile their loss with religious beliefs. 'If there is a god then why did he do this to me, to my child?' they ask. At times like this it is easy to see why even the most religious of people suddenly lose their faith. I think that one of the problems is that we tend to view death as a punishment because we cannot believe that there is a place better than this. But if we come to believe in an afterlife, and come to understand that this afterlife is better than life here on earth, then we could view an early death as not a punishment but a reward. Our lives are fated and we are all living out our destiny here. As wrong as it seems, the simple fact is that some of us are meant to go young. We are put on this earth for a reason and when we have fulfilled that role we can leave this world behind.

I do believe that there are some people here on earth who are angels. When I say angels I am not talking about wings, halos and harps! I mean good people, people who are really special. These people always put others first and radiate love and happiness whatever their state of mind. They are the ones who only have to walk into a room for people to at once feel happy and secure. I believe that these people were sent into our lives for that reason. They were sent to us to enrich our lives, to make us happy, to give us hope. They have not only touched our lives, but they have made this world, our world, a better place.

These people come into our lives for a brief time, maybe only a couple of years, but have such a profound effect on us that their loss is almost too much to bear. I believe that God lends us these people, albeit for a short time, to help us. They are angels because they are carrying out his work by showing us compassion, love and peace. They enlighten us emotionally and spiritually. When I sit with a mother whose child has passed over and they tell me of all the good and wonderful things that this child has done I cannot help but think this. 'Why did they have to be taken when they were so wonderful?' they ask me. 'They didn't have a bad bone in their body,' they tell me, and I know from the look in their eyes and the reading I give them that this is the truth. Over the years I have come across many cases like this and what I find interesting is that even if I don't know anything about the person who has passed over, almost instantly in my reading I will be told the same thing time and time again. 'I wasn't meant to stay there,' I'll hear. Or, 'I had done all I could, I had to come back,' they'll say.

As someone with my beliefs and experiences I am never surprised by this. I do think that there are some people who are literally too good for this world. They come here to change our lives for the better and then they are taken from us. Of course I realize as a mother, a wife and a grandmother myself, that this knowledge does little to ease the real pain and loss, but we should not wonder what these people might have done had they lived on, but look at how much they did while we had them.

When I look back at the life of the late Princess of Wales, I believe that she was one of these people. Diana was only human, was by no means perfect, and in many ways was a complex character, but that aside she had so much to offer. Diana's way with people was not just cultivated for the media or the public. Having known her for years she was as kind in private as she was in public. She hated anyone to be upset, or in pain or to be suffering. Whether she was holding a dying child, talking to a man with HIV or worrying about a friend who had simply sprained their ankle, she always treated everyone she met with love and respect. She came into this world and did so much good that when we look back we shouldn't grieve her short life but celebrate such a full one.

NEAR-DEATH EXPERIENCES

It isn't just through my readings that I have got positive proof of the existence of an afterlife. My views on death have been shaped by my own first-hand experience of dying – a phenomenon known as a near-death experience.

A near-death experience happens when people have gone through a physical death, have actually medically 'died' for a couple of minutes or so, and then re-awoken from this state and seemingly 'come back to life'.

You don't have to be a Spiritualist or religious to experience a near death. A near-death experience is a scientific phenomenon whereby the body closes down and can appear to be lifeless, only for the person to emerge from this state alive. In recent years there has been a great deal of research into this area with scientists and doctors trying to establish what happens to the individual during this time – both physically and mentally. What is perhaps fascinating about this research and other near-death stories is that the people who have been through this experience all have a similar tale to tell afterwards. Even those who had not believed in an afterlife, in god or were in fact completely atheist described the same scenario.

After their 'death' they described how they were able to leave their body, how they sat upright and moved away from the scene, unable to communicate or get the attention of those around them. They talk of having an out-of-body experience – how they were able to look down on their body, and how they moved away. They describe being drawn towards a bright dazzling pinhole of light. The nearer they got to it the larger it became, as though they were moving down a tunnel of darkness towards a brilliant white light. For some the experience ended here, and they felt as though they were being sucked away from the tunnel, waking later to find that they were back in their bodies. However, for some the experience goes further. They talk about reaching the end of the tunnel and arriving at a place full of brightness. They met family members or friends who had passed away and were told to go back. They then also speak of being pulled away from the light and coming round, waking up, in this world.

Some people suggest that these experiences are nothing more than dreams. However, what I find interesting is that the research and my own dealings with near-death experiences and the stories from around the world all recount the same things. Perhaps my own interest in this subject stems from my own near-death experience seventeen years ago.

It happened when I was still living in Mansfield. Following a long period of extreme stress I suffered a mild heart attack. The night it happened Mo and I had been to a local dance but I had not been feeling well all evening. When we got home I felt incredibly drained and weak. I thought that a cup of hot sweet tea might make me feel better so I went to the kitchen to put the kettle on, but as soon as I got into the kitchen I was gripped by an acute pain in my chest. I felt as though my heart was being squeezed, and that it was on fire. I stood there doubled up and gasping, unable to cry out, then unable to stand any longer and fell to the floor. By the time that Mo had come looking for me I was lying on the kitchen floor unconscious.

The strange thing was I didn't realize I was unconscious.

What I remember was suddenly sitting upright. I felt fine and the pain had disappeared. I stood up and walked towards the door – I think I must have been looking for Mo. I turned back and to my surprise saw him kneeling on the floor trying to administer first aid to a woman who was lying there. He was pummelling her chest and crying. I couldn't think who she was. I tried to call out to ask him what was going on but he couldn't hear me. To my amazement I heard him say, 'Rita, please don't die!' I realized that the woman lying on the floor was in fact me. I was looking down on myself. I must have passed over, I thought to myself. The peculiar thing was that I didn't feel 'dead'. I felt full of life, light and young. I was without pain and if the truth be told felt better than I had done in years.

At that moment I felt as though I was suddenly being wrenched and pulled from where I stood in the kitchen. I was being pulled so quickly that I couldn't really see where I was but I seemed to be travelling down a very dark tunnel, heading towards a pinpoint of bright light. I don't remember feeling scared, frightened or indeed sad. As I got nearer to the light and it became brighter and brighter I kept hearing my name being called over and over again, 'Rita, Rita,' a softly spoken chant by a chorus of voices. As I reached the end of the tunnel I was pulled into this dazzling brilliant white light and I was overwhelmed by this great feeling of joy.

The bright light seemed to melt away before my eyes and I found myself standing, though I could feel nothing concrete under my feet, in front of this beautiful landscape filled with rolling hills, hedgerows, trees and flowers. It was like a dream. There was a luminous light as though it were a summer's day and

I could see people strolling about in the distance. A hedgerow separated me from this idyllic scene and against a gate stood my Grandma Alice, my first husband Dennis and my aunts Ivy and Lizzie. They had come to meet me and I remember feeling very happy, hoping that they would open the gate and let me come to them. But they wouldn't. It was Dennis who spoke to me. 'Rita,' he said. 'You're not dead, you must go back.' And at that moment, before I had a chance to speak to him, I felt myself being sucked back through the dark tunnel. As I came out of the tunnel and fell gently to my feet I was once again back in my kitchen. Without any thought I automatically walked towards my body, lay down and re-entered myself. Then I blacked out.

The next thing I recall was coming round. I felt hazy and sore, but the stabbing pain had gone. Mo was above me still pummelling my chest. As I came to Mo breathed a sigh of relief. 'You're back!' he said. 'Thank God for that.' I was back. To all intents and purposes nothing had changed – except my outlook, that is!

3. *The Invisible Detectives*

Spirits begin their communication with me in readings by talking to me about the circumstances that surrounded their deaths. This can be a very harrowing experience not just for me but more importantly for the person I am reading for. Sometimes I will have to take a decision as to whether the information the spirit is giving me is helpful for the person I am reading for and whether this information should be passed on. I may have to spare the family or friend the most distressing details of what I am being told and concentrate instead on the fact that the spirit is now happy, safe and well, and without pain.

Spirits pass this information on to me not only to establish and prove to the person who has come for the reading that I am indeed communicating with them but also because it is a means of reassurance. Spirits want you to know that however painful, harrowing or violent their death was they are now free of pain and are able to talk about it.

Another reason why spirits pass on this information is that there are usually many unanswered questions and grey areas about death. Even if we were with our loved one in their final moments here on the earth plane we do not always know what they were thinking or feeling. We may not have had a chance to say goodbye. We may want to know how much they suffered or whether they were at peace when their time finally came. Even in the most peaceful of passings, people still come to me and ask these questions. The communication that I have with the spirit world, the messages that the spirits give me, enable me and the recipients of those messages to make sense of the many unanswered questions that surround a person's death.

In my experience such messages can be extremely helpful to those who have been left behind, particularly in cases where there have been question marks over the death, such as in incidents of suicide or murder. A reading can help piece together the final moments of a life and answer questions that an inquest, a pathology or hospital report never can. In this way I like to think that spirits act as investigators, solving mysteries only they have the answers for, which is why I call spirits my invisible detectives.

Sometimes the messages that come my way are not clear. Sometimes I am not even sure what they mean. I may see a symbol or hear a word in my head that means nothing to me but when I repeat this to the person I am reading for it makes sense to them. Spirits like to be quite precise because they want to prove to you that you are actually in communication with them. I recently, for example, read for the mother of a boy in spirit who told me that his name was Zack. He was very keen for me to tell her that it was 'Zack as in Zachary and not Zachariah'!

By giving me initials, names, facts and specific details the spirit is trying to present to you a picture of what happened to them, and perhaps an explanation of why it happened too. Even though, more often than not, I will find myself helping to piece together some mystery as a result of a reading, I don't like to claim to be some psychic detective because it is, after all, the spirits who are giving me the information. I am simply the channel through which the spirits answer your questions.

ACCIDENTAL DEATH

The problem with accidents is that they seem so pointless, so meaningless. We are not conditioned to believe that a child with a bright future, who has done well at school, is well liked and shows so much potential should have their life cut short in a car accident. It seems to us wrong that a young mother and her children should be killed in a fire. Or that a middle-aged man who had fought off cancer for the past ten years should then lose his life in a plane crash.

In all these incidences we are left asking 'why?' Even with the answers at our disposal we still cannot make sense of it and this I find tends to affect the way we look at the rest of our lives. This is certainly what happened in the following story. Sally came my way a few years ago. Her son had been killed in an accident abroad. She had never been able to accept what had happened and this in turn affected her outlook, her relationship with her family and also I believe had slowed down her grieving process. Here she tells her story in her own words.

My son James was killed in an accident some years ago. He was in his early twenties and had been studying Philosophy at university. He had gone abroad with a friend for the summer holidays when he was killed in a meaningless accident. One of the worst things about his death is that we were not able to say goodbye to him. To make this tragedy all the more traumatic we were not able to get his body back to England for three weeks. This made the wait for his funeral very hard. I never in my life have suffered from so much pain. Nothing can make up for the loss of a child. I tried to make sense of his death but just wasn't able to. For a time I wanted to die myself but realized that this was selfish because I have other children and it was not something that James would have wanted. So I try to get on with my life, but not a day goes by when I don't think of him and long for him to be back with us.

We didn't really know much about the accident. My husband and I went to the place where it had happened in Spain but because neither of us speaks a word of Spanish we found it quite frustrating. We couldn't get the answers we needed.

On the night of his death James had been out with his friend in a bar. The friend had met up with a girl who he was interested in and had left James at the bar to go on to a night club. James was happy in the bar but had agreed to meet up with them later on. When he eventually left the bar at around 1 a.m. instead of walking to the club, or getting a taxi, he got on the back of another friend's moped. They turned on to the main road but were hit by an on-coming jeep full of young people. All the people involved in the accident were seriously injured but only James died. According to the reports he survived the actual crash but died hours later on the way to hospital. Because I didn't know any of the young people he was with I have never really understood what exactly happened. I wanted to know about the last few hours of his life. I wanted to know whether he was having a good time and also, perhaps more importantly, to what degree he had suffered.

For a long time I dealt with my pain on my own, and had never discussed any of these issues with anyone. After the funeral and the inquest my husband and I never brought the matter up again. I think he didn't want to broach the subject because he thought it might make my grief worse, but there wasn't a day when these questions didn't go through my mind.

About eighteen months ago I decided to write to Rita Rogers and ask her opinion. I mentioned in my letter that I had lost my son. I didn't say how. I just said it was abroad and that I wanted to know whether he was happy now. I think I was looking for peace of mind.

I knew that Rita had a good reputation and that she would be able to reassure me but I was not prepared for how much detail she was going to provide me with. As soon as the reading began she said she had a young male with her and she said his initial was J. She told me he had come with another boy called Mark. She then told me the J she was talking to was a James. She did not tell me who the Mark was but I assumed that it was a school friend of James' who had died in a boating accident years before.

She told me that James had died in Spain, that she could see a crash site and mangled bike. She said she saw other people, they were bleeding and there was a lot of confusion. She said they had turned into a main road from a lane when a jeep, which was going too fast, hit them. She said there was screaming and then quiet. She then said the most unbelievable thing. She said, 'It was no one's fault, it was going to happen anyway. My time had come. You must stop blaming the others.' It is true I had been resentful of the others who had survived the crash. It's awful to admit but sometimes I wondered why it had to be my son and not someone else's child. But as if this wasn't enough Rita said, 'Stop blaming Marco.' Marco had been the boy riding the bike that James had been on. Although there was no evidence that he had been over the limit I am afraid to say that I had never believed this to be true. Hurt and angered by the stupidity of my son's death I was desperate to appropriate the blame on to some one.

Rita assured me that James had not been in pain. She told me that he lost consciousness when he hit the road because he wasn't wearing a helmet, which was true. She also said that he was telling me how happy he was now, how he was with my father, who I lost when I was a child, and Mark.

The reading didn't bring my son back to me but it did lay to rest some emotions that I think were preventing me from being able to grieve properly. It has helped in so many ways and has improved the relationships I have with my other children and my husband.

Sally's reading helped her to get over her feelings of resentment and anger, and that in turn allowed her to confront her grief and loss. Not knowing how someone has died, and what happened to them before, during and after the accident can be extremely difficult to bear, and I think can be dangerous because these emotions stop us from letting go, and of facing up to the reality of what has happened. In short, the unsolved mystery of the death makes us live in the past instead of the present or the future because we are constantly reliving that event in our minds. Resentment and anger are not the only emotions that are triggered from accidental deaths: it is common for the person left behind to suffer from an extreme and irrational sense of guilt too, even though they had nothing to do with the events leading up to the accident.

I received a letter from a woman a while ago who had lost

her husband. She was terribly upset and said that when she was with her friends she put a brave face on but deep down she missed him very much. She was worried though that her husband might be angry with her and that she suffered from terrible nightmares. In the letter she did not elaborate on why he might be angry with her, but that she was worried and felt that she could no longer cope.

Despite my large mailbag of requests for readings I knew that I had to give this poor woman a reading because grief is hard enough to bear without feelings of guilt keeping one up at night.

I called her one morning and agreed to read for her. Immediately her father-in-law came to me in spirit and sent her all his love. He told me his name, which the woman told me was correct. He said that he was with the woman's husband and they were there in spirit together.

Then the husband came through to me. He was sending out this huge feeling of warmth and was telling me how much he loved his wife. He named his children and sent them his love. He told me that they had all moved house since he passed away. And that he was proud of his grandson.

He named two of the woman's friends who had passed away, the names of her parents who were there with him in spirit and that he was also with the family cat!

He went on to say that his 'time had come', and was telling me to tell her not to blame herself. He kept repeating the phrase 'my time had come' over and over as if he was making a point. He knew that she was upsetting herself because of what had happened but he wanted her to know that it was nothing to do with her.

He told me they had been swimming together. The woman had got out of her depth and he had tried to save her. While he was doing this he suffered a heart attack which killed him. He didn't know then he had a heart condition but he knew now that the heart attack would have happened sooner or later because his time had come.

By the end of the reading I knew that I had helped the woman. She hadn't told me how he had died before the reading so she knew I must be telling the truth. Whilst I might not be able to stop her grieving for her soulmate, I knew the reading would stop her from punishing herself with feelings of guilt.

ILLNESSES

The suffering of a loved one can cause those left behind terrible distress. We really want to know how much they suffered during their illness and at the time of their death, whether they were in pain or not, and whether they are still suffering. One thing I can say for sure is that no matter how bad the suffering has been here on earth you can guarantee that anyone who has passed away and has entered the spirit world is no longer in pain. As I said earlier we are all perfect in spirit. Of course saying this to people is sometimes just not enough, they really do need to know that I am communicating with the spirit of the one who has passed over before they can be reassured, as this next story shows. It has been written by Sarah, a mother who lost her son to leukaemia.

My son Stephen died last year. He was only seventeen. My husband, Greg, and I were devastated at losing him. Although he had been very sick for some time and in much pain this didn't make it any easier for us. A lot of people said to us when he died that it was for the best and that at last he was at peace. Whilst I knew there was truth in this, and that they meant well, this did little to comfort my husband or me. The fact is we had lost our boy and we were inconsolable.

I had heard of Rita Rogers through a friend who had read one of her books and had seen her talking about her work on the television. Although Greg and I believed in an afterlife, both having Christian upbringings, we had never considered seeing a medium before, but my friend explained how Rita specialized in helping people who had lost children so I decided to write to her.

In the letter I explained that we had lost a child. I only told her his name and age, and asked whether it would be possible in the future to talk to her about Stephen. I wasn't sure if Rita could help us but it was worth a shot. Greg and I had so many things that were preying on our minds. We wondered whether Stephen had been aware that we were there with him when he died. We desperately wanted to know whether he was OK or whether he was still in pain. Most of all we wanted to tell him how much we all missed him.

I never thought that I would get a reply but some weeks later I received a call and an appointment was made. I was given a date to call Rita for a reading.

Rita was very friendly on the telephone and that put me at ease. I had been very nervous about speaking to her. I was worried that she might not be able to tell me anything about Stephen or that she might not even make contact with him at all. As it was my concerns were unfounded.

Almost immediately Rita told me that Stephen had come through to her. She knew that he had passed away because I had told her in my letter but what was amazing is that she said that he was with his grandmother, Helen, who she named. This was incredibly comforting to me. I guess like any parent who has lost a child we were worried that Stephen, wherever he was, was alone. She told me that Helen was telling her that she had passed away with a heart condition and wanted to send her love to my father Philip, who again Rita named.

Rita then said that Stephen was talking to her. He was telling her that he had been ill for a very long time and had suffered from a blood problem. She then came out with leukaemia. I didn't say anything because to be honest I was too stunned. Rita said that he was sending his love to his sisters Caroline and Lucy. I knew then that Rita really was talking to our son.

What was wonderful about the reading is that Rita said that Stephen was no longer in pain. He was telling her that he knew that we had all been there when he eventually passed away, that we had played music. This was nice for us because Stephen wasn't conscious when he went. We had been frightened that he didn't realize how much we loved him and that we were all there for him.

There were other details that Rita gave us that really made us believe that she was genuinely talking to Stephen and that there must be an afterlife. She told us, for example, that we had given flowers to the nurses who had cared for Stephen, which was true, and that my eldest daughter was having a baby. No stranger could have made any of these things up. The most incredible thing she said was that she knew that I took his favourite toy bear with me whenever we went away.

These may seem like small things to other people but to a parent it's these little things that convince you that there is an afterlife and that your child is still with you. We know now that Stephen is at peace and out of pain and so when people say this to us now, we actually understand what they mean.

UNDERSTANDING SUICIDE

Whilst it can seem, at the time, a solution to those in despair, in trouble, or in deep depression, the act of suicide always causes more suffering than it heals. The people left behind endure the most terrible pain. Pain not just at losing their loved ones and the grief that goes hand in hand with that loss, but the pain of thinking they could or should have done something to prevent the suicide. With that particular pain come feelings of guilt, anger and betrayal, emotions that some people never recover from. The ones left behind become as much the victim as the person who took their own life.

The readings I do for people who have lost their loved ones to suicide are always extremely clear and strong. When the person who has taken their own life reaches the spirit world they see and understand how much grief their action has caused. They realize the hurt and the pain that they have created, and they are desperate to make amends for this.

So keen are they to make up for the suffering they have caused that in some cases I find that spirits of suicide cases go out of their way to bring their loved ones to readings with me. One woman came to me via a very roundabout way after her husband died. She had gone to a bookshop to buy a friend a cookery book as a birthday present, but she found herself being drawn to a shelf that stocked books on Mind, Body and Soul. There on the shelf amongst hundreds of other books she saw a copy of *From One World to Another*, picked it up, took it to the counter and without even flipping through it or studying the jacket she paid for it. Later that night she wrote to me asking for a reading. She still hadn't read the book, she had never heard of me, but a voice in her head was telling her to contact me.

Months later I gave her a telephone reading during which her husband who had taken his own life came through. He told me to tell her he loved her, that he was sorry, that it wasn't her fault and that he was looking after her. He also said that it had been him who had led her to me. He described taking her in to the shop and had wanted her to write to me so that he could say this in the reading. This story was all the more remarkable given that the lady lived in Australia.

In my experience, however, we sometimes mistakenly categorize deaths as suicides when they were simply accidents. Whilst a lot of people full of despair make a cry for help it is only ever a small percentage who actually intend to go through with it and succeed.

One reason why we often mistake an accidental death for a suicide is that in some cases there just isn't enough evidence to prove that the death happened in any another way. At a loss to explain why the death occurred it is assumed that the people concerned have taken their own lives, as the next story shows.

Jason, an architect in his early thirties, had been deeply in love with his boyfriend Chris. They had been with each other for a couple of years and they didn't need me to tell them that they were soulmates. Not only was there a deep physical attraction between them but as characters they got on extremely well. Whilst Jason was quite outgoing and ambitious, Chris was more sensitive and thoughtful, but this combination of personalities worked well together.

Jason had been aware right from the start of their relationship that Chris was prone to depression but he saw this as part of the sensitive side of his character and didn't worry about it too much. Chris had been prescribed various courses of anti-depressants and during their two years together everything seemed to be fine. One weekend towards the end of the summer Jason was sent away to Brussels on business. Jason recalled afterwards that although everything seemed OK at home, for some reason he had a feeling that he shouldn't leave Chris alone in the flat in London that weekend. Chris had told him not to be so silly when Jason repeated this to him. He was used to Jason having to go away at weekends, and in any case he had lots to do around the house and on Saturday night he had made plans to see some friends. So Jason made the trip.

On Sunday morning at around 5.30 a.m. Jason got a call on his mobile from a friend with some tragic news. Chris was dead. He had thrown himself out of a window. He had taken his own life. Feeling completely numb Jason took the next plane back to London. He couldn't understand what had happened. He couldn't believe that Chris would do this to himself. Even at his lowest ebb Chris was not the kind of person who would do this to himself or others around him.

For months after that Jason went through turmoil. At first he blamed himself for not reading the signs. Later he wondered whether he really knew the man he had spent the last two years of his life with. He then began to ask himself whether Chris had ever loved him.

Jason was so tortured about what was going on that he eventually made an appointment to see me, which he later admitted was completely out of character.

Although I didn't know why this young man was here for a reading, as soon as he walked through the door I felt Chris's presence. I didn't have to call for him to come to me. It was as though he had accompanied Jason to the reading. I told Jason that I had Chris with me and that he was telling me his name and that he was Jason's boyfriend. He then took me through what happened on the night of his death. He told me where he had been, where Jason was and which friends he had been with earlier that evening.

Chris was suddenly talking to me very quickly. He was desperate to get something across as soon as he could. He was telling me that he had taken a fatal cocktail of drugs. He had taken antidepressants and later on that night he had drunk a lot and later taken a cocktail of recreational drugs. This combination was to prove fatal. By the time he got home that evening he was hot and high. He opened the French windows of his flat and stood on the balcony. He thought he could fly and decided to stand on top of the edge of the balcony and throw himself off.

Jason knew that I was telling the truth because he knew that there was no way I could have made any of this up. I had described to him exactly the events of the night, named their friends, and correctly told him that Chris had jumped from the French windows of their second-floor flat. This message came from no one other than Chris and he wanted to tell his lover, his soulmate, that he had not intentionally killed himself, that it was an accident. There were other things that were said during the reading, small details, secrets that only they shared, that convinced Jason that Chris would never have left him like that. That he had made a mistake. Weeks later Jason wrote to tell me how much the reading had helped him and that it allowed him to come to terms with Chris's death.

MISSING PEOPLE

I have always maintained that not knowing can often be worse than the truth. Not knowing the whereabouts of your child, whether your mother is alive and well, or where your husband has disappeared to can often be far harder to deal with than if you knew that they were dead. When a person passes over you can at least mourn them, you can lay their spirit to rest, celebrate their life and try to move on. In the case of a missing person you cannot do any of this. Your life is left in limbo. You wait for the moment they will walk through the door again. You cannot mourn them, you cannot give up hope, and you just have to keep waiting.

Readings with those who have lost people can be productive because your spirit guides see the agony that you are suffering and try their best to help you. Our spirits are there to protect and guide us, and I often find that when I am reading for a missing person these spirits are often making it their mission to help you to find your loved one. As I discovered last year when I read for a lady in South Africa whose daughter had gone missing from boarding school.

It had been three months since the thirteen-year-old's disappearance and everybody feared the worst – including the local papers who were posting 'missing presumed dead' notices all over the area.

During the lady's reading the girl's grandmother had a different story to tell. She came through at once, so full of news and information that I thought that I was never going to get a word in edgeways. She told me of a young girl who had been unhappy at school for some time. She described her grand-daughter as a country girl who had many friends back at home and liked nothing more than riding around her area on her bike, but when she arrived at her new private school she hadn't fitted in. She had no friends, was lonely and bullied. She would have confided in her brother but he was now living in London. She felt that she couldn't tell her parents about how miserable she was because they had paid so much money for her to go there and had been so proud when she had been accepted by the school.

Not knowing where to turn and feeling very down about her life the troubled teenager had run away from school one afternoon. Her grandmother was showing her cycling on her bike away from the gates. (This was in fact how she left the school that afternoon.) She told me that the girl had met a group of New Age travellers sited within a thirty-mile radius of her home. They had made friends with her and allowed her to stay with them.

'Follow the river' was the message I was told to pass on to the girl's mother during the reading. So having consulted a map the girl's mother did exactly this and sure enough found the travellers' camp.

Her daughter wasn't there but she met several people, witnesses, who attested to seeing her daughter and vouched for her well-being. She had with her a photograph of her daughter and was told that her daughter had been with them for a couple of weeks, that she was happy and well but had decided to move on.

I didn't reunite mother and daughter, perhaps they still weren't ready for that, but the mother was at least consoled by the fact that although her daughter was still missing she was happy, well and most importantly of all alive.

Finding a person who has been lost or has gone missing is one of the most rewarding aspects of my work, especially if they are found alive and well. However, I cannot guarantee that if they are found they *are* going to be alive and well. Sadly this is not always the case. Breaking bad news to someone who has come to see me in the hope that I might find their loved one is always very difficult. But, as I said earlier, in the long run it is better to know because it means that the waiting can end and we can finally lay them to rest.

Last spring I received a letter from America that bothered me. It was from a woman called Nancy who had lost her brother twelve years earlier in what she described as tragic circumstances. She wrote that it had happened abroad. It wasn't that she had lost her brother that concerned me most, but that the body of her brother had never been recovered.

'My mother has obviously suffered greatly,' she wrote. 'And even though we know that he must be dead, I think she sometimes thinks that one day he will walk through the door.'

The woman ended her brief letter by saying that they would

be 'very comforted with any sort of contact at all'.

This was one letter I could not ignore and agreed to a reading straight away. Losing people is very hard, but in cases like this one, the worst aspect is the not knowing. I understood the mother's anguish entirely and I empathized with her belief that her son might one day reappear.

When we lose someone suddenly, especially if they are young, or our child, it is difficult to accept that it is true. It never really sinks in. In many respects funerals can be helpful because we have to accept what has happened *has* happened. They become a focus. By confronting a coffin, by going to a service, by saying goodbye, we come face to face with reality – however painful that is.

This family had spent the last twelve years in the dark and in some ways that is even more difficult to come to terms with. Not only is there the mystery of what happened to the person, but also with that comes the inability to grieve, to lay things to rest. In short, people in these situations are left in the most awful state of emotional limbo, with no chance of closure.

As soon as Nancy's reading began her brother came to me. He told me that his name was Tony and he wanted Nancy to know that he had not taken his own life. He was with his grandmother and also with his friend, Seth, who I felt had died with him. Tony was taking me to South America, to a place near mountains. He was telling me how much he loved to travel and see new places, and there was something adventurous about his nature. I felt that when he was at home working in New York he had been saving every penny so that he could travel. He loved the countryside and wildlife.

Tony began telling me that he and Seth had been walking on the day they died. A jeep drove past filled with men wearing bandannas on their heads. They were holding guns. Tony told me that they shot at them as they drove by. He said that both he and Seth died instantly. The men then took Tony's watch and money, which had been in a money belt. This all took place near a river.

Tony told me he knew Nancy had been thinking of retracing his steps but that he didn't want her to go alone. If she must make the trip she should take a guide and follow the river to the mountains. He was showing me a picture of bushes near this river. I believe that he showed me this image because that is where his body had been left.

The information that Tony had given me had been very detailed and it seemed to make sense to Nancy, but the most important message was that he had not suffered. He was in the wrong place at the wrong time was his message. The people who had taken his life had been bandits with no humanity.

In a reading like this, one always hopes, and by that I mean *both* the sitter and myself, that there will be good news. There is nothing that I would like more, particularly where there is any doubt, than to turn to the person and say, 'your child is still alive'. But in this case I think that Nancy and even her mother knew that this would not happen. They knew in their heart of hearts that Tony had passed over. But what was good was that at least now they knew he hadn't suffered, that they could cherish his memory and at last mourn him. His final words to me were that he loved them all and that he still travelled in spirit.

*

The messages I get from the spirit world can often help people come to terms with what they already know. In traumatic situations the mind and body are great shock absorbers. Sometimes we bury difficult memories deep in our subconscious in order to protect ourselves. Readings are helpful for people in these circumstances because they can unearth some of those repressed memories and shed light on a mystery that deep down we know the answer to.

Some years ago I read for a young woman who in the interest of security I am going to rename Emma. When Emma rang me all I knew was that she had lost her mother because right at the start of the reading she said to me, 'I'd love to hear from my mother.'

She was in luck that day because as the reading began her mother came through, told me her name and sent Emma all her love.

'You have a brother don't you?' I said to her. 'I can see you both as children, you lived in America.'

'That's right,' she said.

'And your father . . . John, he lived in America too.'

'Yes,' she said. So far the reading was progressing in the usual way. I was picking up names and a picture of Emma and her family, telling her about her job, her brother and so on. But then all of a sudden the whole nature of the reading changed. Her mother was trying to tell me something. It was something dreadful. At first I wasn't quite sure if I had heard her correctly, but she repeated it again. 'Oh my God!' I said to Emma, taken aback. 'Your mother's telling me she was murdered.'

Through the sobbing at the end of the telephone Emma said to me, 'I *knew* she was!'

'It happened in water didn't it,' I said, as this horrific story was unfolded to me in my mind's eye.

'Yes it did,' she replied almost in a whisper.

'It was your father,' I told her.

'I know,' was her reply.

Emma's father was a perfectionist who was prone to violent fits and rages. He would often hit his wife and sometimes push her around. As a child Emma and her brother had grown up against this backdrop of fighting and screaming.

As the reading progressed Emma's mother was giving me a clear picture of the events of the night that she died. I asked Emma if she wanted to go on with the reading. Her mother seemed keen for me to tell Emma what had happened but I had to make sure that Emma was ready for it. 'Please go on,' she said. 'We need to know that we were right.'

I focused my mind on Emma's mother again. 'Your father is in the bathroom, they had a row . . . a terrible argument . . . she was going to leave.' The message I was getting in my head from Emma's mother was no longer just a voice. I could now see what had happened in my mind. 'She said she was leaving him,' I continued. 'But he wasn't having it. He stormed upstairs. She had gone into the bathroom to run a bath, threw a few things into a bag and then got into the tub,' I said. 'But he just barged in. She shouted at him to get out, he wouldn't, in one hand he held a hairdryer, he switched it on and threw it into the bath. It killed her. You and your brother saw it. But you were not sure about it. You were too young to know what was going on,' I said.

Emma was only five years old when this happened. Her brother was just seven. They had heard their parents fighting that night. Her brother remembers their mother saying that she was going to leave. The children had been on the landing outside the bathroom door, which was ajar. They remembered their father throwing something into the bath. They remember being told the following day that their mother was dead. Their father had said there had been an accident. He took them to live in Europe after that and brought them up away from their mother's family.

After the reading I asked Emma if she was OK. 'Oh yes,' she said. 'I wanted this reading because I needed to know if my brother and I had been right all these years. In a strange way I still love my father, we speak on the telephone but we don't see him now. He is in America now and is old,' she explained. 'I don't want to punish him. I know my mother wouldn't want that either because I believe that when he dies he will get whatever he deserves then.'

4. The Missing Link

Whether it is retracing the final moments of someone's life, locating an important document or passing on a simple message of love or forgiveness, the messages I receive from the spirit world, as I have shown in the last two chapters, can really help the people left behind.

The majority of people who come to me for a reading do so because they have questions they need answering. I will get a letter from a father who still cannot make sense of his daughter's suicide; from a wife who does not understand why the doctors could not save her husband's life or a call from a mother simply asking why her child was taken from her at such a young age. These are questions that sometimes parents, doctors or the police cannot answer and so people turn to me for help. As I have explained earlier these questions are answered during a reading because spirits love us and want to help us. They hate to see us suffer.

When other more orthodox and traditional channels of enquiry fail, when all leads have been exhausted, people come to me for answers. I am turned to, usually as a last resort, to help shed light or possibly solve a mystery.

Over the past thirty years I have been involved in helping the police, the army and the British media on a number of cases which have ranged from locating lost or missing people, to finding the bodies of people who have been involved in accidents or foul play, to unearthing new and crucial evidence in murder cases. I have even helped out in a kidnap case. By acting as a channel between this world and the next I can help people find what they are looking for.

Although I am always keen to help people I cannot say that this aspect of the work I do is easy. I always think carefully before I commit myself to a case.

Firstly, I have to ask myself whether I am up to the job or not, if I am physically strong enough to do it. A lot of these cases can be extremely harrowing especially when dealing with violent crime, murder or abuse. The spirit who is guiding me may be the victim of that crime, so I have to be aware that if I make contact with them they may take me through their ordeal during the reading. Secondly, I have to consider whether I am mentally and emotionally up to it. Like anyone else I suffer from bad days: I may not be feeling well; I may be stressed about something or be upset. All these states of mind affect how sensitive I am and can result in a bad reading. In a normal situation I would postpone an appointment until I was feeling better, but in a case where time is of the essence this cannot always happen.

Furthermore, in this job you have to be responsible. You can't just say things because you know that's what people want to hear. If you have bad news then it is your duty to pass it on and to do that sensitively. In my work you always have to be 100 per cent sure of what you are saying – even if you are simply passing on a name or an initial during a reading. There is no room for guesswork in this business. You have to be completely certain and confident that what you are saying is right simply because the smallest mistake or ambiguity could jeopardize the case, and put the police off the right trail. You may be wasting valuable time, or giving a person hope when there is none to be had.

The fourth thing to remember is that in situations like these people are coming to me as a last resort when all other routes and leads have failed. So I always have to be aware of their state of mind. They are usually at the end of their tether, and are desperate for new information. They are at their most vulnerable – and in my experience people who are vulnerable are at their most impressionable. However tempted you are to help people, you cannot say something that is not true. If nothing comes to me, I will have to tell them so and that can be very difficult, because they are counting on me, grasping at straws, looking to me for hope.

The final point to make is that no matter how much reliable information you give to a family, to the police or the media, one has to remember that they can only ever take it as a lead. No matter how good the psychic's reputation is, what they say can never be used as evidence in a court of law. You can only give people a lead and hope that they will follow it up. It is up to the authorities to find evidence to support the information.

For this reason many of the cases I have been, or am currently, involved with cannot be written about, either because they are still in the process of being examined or because it can be dangerous for the people involved or for myself. Moreover, most of the time the police are understandably reluctant to go on the record to say that they have used psychics. While there are a great many people who would be prepared to turn to a psychic for help, there are as many people who would feel uneasy about that kind of thing.

People often come to me thinking I have all the answers. I don't. I can only do my best to help. But often by communicating with the spirit world, by acting as a missing link, I can help to find new information that may solve a mystery.

MISSING PEOPLE

There are two ways in which I use my gift to help locate a missing person. If the person I am trying to locate is still alive, then I will receive guidance either from my own spirit guide or from someone close to them in the spirit world. If the person I am looking for comes through to me, and I can hear them in my inner ear, it means that they have passed over. In some cases when the person has passed over, they may not come through to me immediately – this usually happens in situations when the death has been very recent and they have not yet ascended into the spirit world. It may take a couple of readings and some time before I get them in spirit, and can therefore be certain that they have passed over.

The procedure for finding a missing person is the same as for a normal reading. I will ask a member of the person's family or one of their friends to come to me or call me for a reading. I do this so I am able to focus on the missing person and provide a link between this world and the spirit world.

I may ask the person coming for the reading to bring something that belongs to the missing person, something personal – like a watch or a piece of jewellery, to help me focus on the missing person. The vibrations given off by the jewellery help me to concentrate and give me a clearer picture of what the person is like and where they might be. In cases of missing people this can be helpful because if they are still alive I will not get them in spirit, so I need all the help I can get to sense where they are.

In *From One World to Another* I described the story of how I was once called on by the army to locate two soldiers who had vanished in a blizzard in the Cairngorm mountains in Scotland. I had been telephoned in desperation by their Major who asked if I could help locate them. He reminded me that I had read for one of the soldiers many years ago and that I had predicted that one day he would be 'lost in snow'. I agreed to help, and the father of the other lost soldier came to me for a reading. Almost immediately I sensed that his son was still alive and I pinpointed the spot where I believed he had made a shelter on the mountainside, which surprised even me since I have never been to the Cairngorms!

An army helicopter was sent to the site I had described but unfortunately, because of the harsh weather conditions, it was not able to land. By the following day when they did manage to land, it was too late and both soldiers had perished. To the amazement of the helicopter pilot, who had been very sceptical of my involvement in the operation, the soldiers were in the exact location I had predicted.

I have handled many missing person cases over the years. For example, I have located the whereabouts of a lost teenage girl in Ireland, found the body of a murdered child in a lake, traced a husband who had left his family and moved to Canada. But it was to be the Cairngorm story which led me, sixteen years later, to one of the most difficult and high-profile cases of my career: the search for Ben Needham, the little boy who vanished from Kos, in Greece, ten years ago.

For a number of reasons I have decided not to write about my involvement in the search for Ben in 1991. My part in the case was controversial, and for copyright reasons and out of respect for the Needham's privacy I cannot go into the content of the reading. Although the search for Ben continues, there is still no sign of the child, but I do believe he is still alive. As a medium, I can only pass on what I hear from the spirit world, and it is up to the people who I read for to interpret that information. I hope that one day I will be able to tell the whole story and, more importantly, that Ben is found. I am convinced that one day we will get to the bottom of that case, but until that time I send out all my love, prayers and hope to the Needham family.

As I have already said, looking for missing people is difficult. I always hope that my reading will help to get to the bottom of the mystery and that the person who has disappeared will be successfully located, but it isn't always that simple. I am not God and I am not a magician. All I can do is try and focus my gift and channel my thoughts and hope, at the very least, that my reading may result in if not the location of the person then in new leads. I can't say I like doing this work, because I hate to shatter hopes and to disappoint, but if I can help people through the agony of their search or even put an end to it, then that's rewarding.

*

One afternoon in the summer of 1998 I was sitting in my chair in my reading room going through my mail. As you can imagine, every day I must receive hundreds of letters from all over the world. With each letter comes a different story: some people are simply looking for a direction in their lives; others want to know when and where they are going to meet their soulmate; and there are those letters which are full of tragedy and despair. Whether they are looking for love, comfort or to make contact with the spirit world all these people are asking for the same thing – my help. This is perhaps the most frustrating aspect of my work because I cannot help everyone who asks for a reading: it would be physically impossible. I already read for ten to fourteen people a week, which I find a strain as it is, and I have a two-year waiting list for appointments. That said, I always make a point of answering letters myself and so, that afternoon, I was sitting in front of a huge pile of envelopes penning my replies. I was about halfway through the pile and feeling quite tired when I suddenly saw an airmail letter. I am not sure why my gaze fixed upon that particular letter, but I just sat there staring at it. It wasn't the only airmail letter, but for some reason it got my attention and I found myself picking it up. It was from America.

With the envelope in my hand I stood up and walked to the window. I still hadn't opened it, but something was urging me to read it. I wasn't sure whether it was my spirit guide or perhaps my grandmother but a faint voice in my head was saying, 'You must help this person, you must read for them.' I found myself tearing open the envelope. It was from Alabama, from a woman called Jackie.

The voice in my head was getting stronger now, louder and clearer. 'Please help her, please help her,' it said over and over. As the voice became more distinct I realized that it wasn't Running Water or my grandmother who was talking to me, it was a young girl. And before I had even read a word I knew that this letter had come from her mother. As I stood there at the window of my reading room clutching the thin sheet of pale-blue writing paper a chill went down my spine. I knew that this was a special case. Whoever had written this letter, and whatever their reason for writing to me, desperately needed my help. Slowly, I began to take in the slanted handwriting – this was a missing persons case: one that involved foul play.

The letter read as follows:

Dear Mrs Rogers

Can you please help me put an end to the suffering, torment and misery that I have had to endure for the past two years? In December of 1996 my daughter Cheryl disappeared. The morning she vanished I got up as usual for work. Having dressed and prepared breakfast for my daughter and my mother who also lived with us, I kissed Cheryl goodbye. She was in high spirits that morning and for once was up before me! The reason for her mood I discovered was the fact that her boyfriend Tommy was due back that evening. He had been away on a trip with some friends and she couldn't wait to see him.

Cheryl is a beautiful and happy girl of African American descent. She was nineteen when she disappeared and was in her second year of college. We all loved her very, very much and were very proud of her.

*That evening when I got back from work Cheryl wasn't there.
I couldn't understand it. She was due to meet Tommy back at our
house at 8 p.m. It was now 7.30 and there was no sign of her. I
asked my mother, who was sitting on our porch, whether she had
seen her. She said not since the morning when Cheryl had left for
work. I decided not to worry, thinking that there must have been a
change of plan, but when Tommy came round to the house half an
hour later and told me he hadn't heard from her and that there
hadn't been a change of plan, I panicked.*

*I called the police, but they said that as she hadn't been
missing for twenty-four hours and was over age there was nothing
that they could do. They asked if she was happy, if we had had a
row. When I said no, they just replied 'Teenagers, you know how
they are.' Twenty-four hours later, when there was still no sign,
and we had searched for her they still did nothing. They made a
note of her name, etc., but they didn't seem to want to search for
her, insinuating that she must have run away. Run away from
what? I keep asking myself. A happy loving family life, a boyfriend
she adored and wanted to marry, and a college life she had worked
so hard for? It didn't, and still doesn't, make sense.*

*I think about her all day and believe that she still is alive. I
have never given up searching and need to find out where she is.
Rita, you are my last hope. Please help me and tell me where she
has gone.*

Jackie

Well, I knew I couldn't ignore this letter. I would try my
best to help Jackie find Cheryl wherever she was. I reached for
the telephone, trying to work out what the time difference was

between England and Alabama. To be honest, I didn't really know where Alabama was – but I reckoned that even if it was early morning there Jackie wouldn't mind if I woke her. After four rings a woman answered. 'Jackie? This is Rita Rogers,' I said. 'Oh Lord!' came the soft voice at the other end of the telephone. 'Thank you, thank you.'

We chatted for several minutes. She told me she had heard of me because a friend of hers had seen me once being interviewed on the *Larry King Show*. She said that she had never imagined that she would get to me, but she gave it a try because she wanted to see someone with a good reputation. Poor Jackie explained how her search for Cheryl had taken her all over the country and how hopeless the authorities had been. I asked her whether she might be able to come and see me for a reading, but she said that this would be impossible since she simply didn't have the funds.

When doing a reading for a missing persons case it is imperative that you have some sort of contact with the person who has disappeared. So I asked Jackie to send me something of Cheryl's, preferably the last thing that she had touched. I warned her not to touch the object too much herself, because that could lessen the effect and I suggested she handled it using a handkerchief.

A week later two parcels arrived, both from Jackie. To my dismay, the first package, which contained a scarf had already been opened by customs officials. I wouldn't be able to get anywhere with that. But, fortunately, the smaller package hadn't been opened. Inside was a pair of gold hoop earrings. There was a note inside explaining that Cheryl had worn these the night before she disappeared.

That afternoon I called Jackie and asked her if she was ready for the reading. She said yes. I could tell by her voice that she was apprehensive, and so was I. I had never done a missing person reading on the telephone like this, I was worried that because the call was long distance it might affect the reading. What if no one came through? What if I could tell Jackie nothing at all?

As it turned out my worries were unfounded because as I sat there in my reading room the telephone in one hand and the earrings in the other, a voice came through loud and clear. It was Jackie's grandmother who was telling me her name, Annie. I asked Jackie if this made sense to her, 'Oh yes,' she said. I could tell her voice was full of hope. But sadly her elation was to be short lived.

Another voice was coming through to me. It was a voice that I recognized, that I had heard the afternoon I had stood at the window with Jackie's letter in my hand. It was Cheryl. My heart sank. How on earth was I going to tell Jackie? Yes, I had found her daughter, but she was not where Jackie wanted her to be. I took a deep breath. I knew I had to tell her, but how?

'Tell her,' Cheryl kept saying. 'She must know.'

I knew she was right. It was my duty to tell the truth and put an end to this woman's agonizing search. 'Cheryl is here with me,' I said gently. 'She has come through, I'm so sorry Jackie,' I said.

There was a long pause and followed by an exhalation of breath. Then there was silence, and then came tears. Cheryl was talking to me in my inner ear. 'I know you are upset Jackie, but Cheryl doesn't want you to be sad, she says she wants you to know that she is safe now and that she loves you.' I asked her if she wanted me to stop. 'Oh no, Rita, you must go on, you must tell me everything,' she said.

I asked Cheryl to take me back to the night that she had disappeared. She told me that after her mother had left for work that morning she had taken a shower. Jackie told me later that this was accurate because when she came back that evening she cursed her daughter for the mess she had left in the bathroom. Cheryl told me then that she worked part time in a restaurant to help pay for her tuition fees. She described the diner which was not far from where she lived. I saw in my mind's eye a large plate-glass window, booths, and a busy kitchen. She showed me her pink and white uniform and told me that she had put it on after her shower. She said that she had been due to start work at 11.30 as she was working the lunchtime shift that day. By now Jackie was in floods of tears. She knew I couldn't be making this up. She knew I was talking to her daughter.

Cheryl was taking me through the day with such precision. I have known spirits to be good with detail, particularly when they are trying to prove something, but I find they are always vague about time, but not in this reading! Cheryl kept giving me specific times – as though she needed to account for every minute. I realized then that she was trying to help her mother build a picture of what had happened, she was proving to her that she was gone and giving her the account of events that led up to death. One the authorities had failed to do.

Cheryl told me that at 11.00 she got a phone call at home from a man who was calling on behalf of her friend Lucy. When I said the name Lucy, I heard Jackie gasp. Lucy was Cheryl's best friend and they had known each other since they were small children. Cheryl was telling me that the man on the other end of the telephone asked if Cheryl could meet Lucy at a motel on her way to work. Cheryl didn't know what it was about, and she didn't know who the man was, but she was so worried that she went anyway. Grabbing her keys and handbag, which I described to Jackie, Cheryl made her way in her car to the motel. She had been told that Lucy would be waiting for her in the motel car park but when she got there, there was no sign of Lucy or her car. It was empty except for an old white van parked in the corner. She pulled into the car park and decided to sit there and wait for her friend. But after twenty minutes and realizing that she should be at work by now, Cheryl decided to check inside the motel. Maybe she was waiting for her there, she thought.

As Cheryl was telling me this images came to me as well. I described the washed-out denim jacket Cheryl wore over her uniform. I told Jackie about the small teddy bear and coloured beads that hung from the rear-view mirror, the empty cans of diet drinks that lay on the floor of the car. Trivial details to anyone else – but to Jackie this was proof that I had made contact with her daughter.

Grabbing her bag and opening the door, about to make her way to the motel, Cheryl was suddenly dealt a blow to the head. Dazed, but not unconscious, a man quickly dragged her across the car park. When they reached the white van another man opened the back door and pulled her inside. Here Cheryl suffered her horrific ordeal.

Breaking news like this to someone you are reading for is very hard. Jackie had already been dealt a dreadful blow and I wasn't sure how much more she could take. I knew the next bit of the reading was going to be difficult for her. As a medium, I work as a messenger from the spirit world to this world, in a sense it's my job to relay everything I hear and not hold things back, but I'm also human. I had just told this woman that she had lost her daughter, was I going to upset her further by going into detail? I asked Jackie how she was feeling and gently explained that I thought that Cheryl was now going to take me through how she had died. I asked her if she wanted to continue, whether we should break off for a while or stop altogether. 'No Rita, you must tell me all of it. I must have the truth, she wants me to know,' she said. And Jackie was right; Cheryl did want her to know.

Cheryl told me that she was raped by the two men that night. She didn't know the one who was holding her down by her wrists the first time it happened but she certainly knew the second man. She gave me his name: Doug. Jackie gasped. 'Oh God, oh God,' she said. I realized then why Jackie was so upset when I said his name: Cheryl was telling me that Doug had been her stepfather.

Later, Jackie explained she had been bowled over by Doug's charm and had fallen for him immediately without knowing him that well. She had hoped that he would become like a father to Cheryl. But Doug had begun to make unwanted advances towards the teenager and it wasn't long before Jackie had thrown him out.

Cheryl told me that she had been raped three times that night. Twice by Doug and once by the other man. She took me to the inside of the van where she lay, her uniform torn from her body. They had stuffed a cloth in her mouth – to dull her screams, I suppose – and she was dozing in and out of consciousness. Once they had finished with her, Doug got her by the neck and strangled her. 'Where is she now?' Jackie whispered. 'Please tell me, I must know.' I shut my eyes and concentrated hard. 'She is in a watery grave,' I said. 'Oh my God,' said Jackie. 'That's what my mother has said all along. She's always been a bit psychic and since Cheryl went, she has sat all day on our porch repeating those words. Watery grave. I didn't know what she meant.'

After Doug had strangled Cheryl the two men had driven the van to a large lake. Having set fire to the remnants of her clothes, they weighed her body down and threw her into the lake. They watched as she slowly sank to the bottom, then they got back into the van and drove away.

Jackie recognized the lake I described, and said she thought she knew who the other man might be. Cheryl had said she wanted her mother to know because she wanted her to end her search. She didn't want her mother to suffer any more, so she needed to know the truth. Sometimes the truth we search for hurts. I knew that Jackie was in pain, but I realized that this truth would put an end to the pain of not knowing. I couldn't have made up the details I had given her, and I know that Jackie knew I must be telling her the truth.

Cheryl's body was never found. The authorities refused to drag the lake. Although Jackie hasn't been able to lay her daughter's body to rest, she has been able to move on. Some months after the reading, Jackie learnt that Doug had been arrested by the police for assaulting and raping an under-age girl. He is now in prison. He may not have paid for his crime against Cheryl, but as I assured Jackie he will do so in the next life.

ON THE MURDER TRAIL

I am sure that some people think being involved in murder cases means I run around crime scenes like some psychic Miss Marple trying to find out who did it! In reality the role I play is far less dramatic. When I work on a murder case I follow exactly the same process as I do in any other reading. I will conduct a reading with a close relative or friend of the victim either in person or on the telephone and, with any luck, will be able to make contact with the spirit of the victim. Sometimes it helps to have a personal object that belonged to the victim, but it is not essential. If I am not able, for whatever reason, to make contact with the victim's spirit then I will communicate with my spirit guide and hope that other spirits close to the victim or the person I am reading for will come to my aid.

Furthermore, it would be quite wrong to suggest that I alone help solve these mysteries. When people come to me, particularly in the case of murder, they do so having been through all the usual channels first. Normally, I am called upon by the family of the victim, but there have been a couple of occasions when the police, exasperated by their own investigations, have turned to me directly, desperate for new leads.

Over the years I have been involved in a number of high-profile murder cases, such as the Newell murders which I wrote about in *From One World to Another*. In some cases the leads I have produced have led indirectly to prosecution. I say indirectly because any lead I give must be supported by evidence that can stand up in court.

These readings can be helpful but it is not a matter of tuning in and getting the answers to your questions straightaway, these things can take some time. What I may think is an irrelevant piece of information can be important, even crucial, to the person I am reading for or the case.

By communicating with the spirit of the victim we can build up a picture of what happened and retrace their final moments. Motive can be established when we look at the victim's private life. Things they may have hidden from us while they were in the world may help us understand why they fell victim to the crime. Even the smallest details can help. I am not just talking about finding evidence, sometimes this information can help the people left behind try and put their lives back together again.

Although in the case that follows, the reading did not lead to the prosecution of the murderer (he was already in prison by the time I did this reading), it did help the victim's mother a great deal. The reading not only answered many questions that the police, forensics and the courts couldn't, more importantly it brought huge comfort to a woman who was in great distress.

In the summer of 2000 I received a letter care of *Bella* magazine asking me for a reading. Given that I must get hundreds letters a week asking for help I am surprised that this one even caught my eye. Maybe the spirits intervened maybe it was chance but somehow the envelope came my way and when I read the short message inside I knew that I had to read for this woman.

In fact the letter didn't say much at all, it was just a couple of lines. Lines that I now know off by heart. It read: 'I lost my daughter last summer, the tears just keep flowing. The whole family is heartbroken, we just don't know when the tears will stop.'

That was all the information I had. I had no idea what the woman's daughter, Laura, had died from and I wouldn't know until Laura told me herself in our reading. All I knew was that I had to speak to her mother, Anne Donnelly, as soon as I could. What I discovered during the reading is the most tragic and horrific story, but one which is also coloured with extreme love, courage and bravery.

On 31 July 1999, Laura Donnelly, a trainee supermarket manager from Paisley, Scotland, was murdered. She was only twenty-two. Following a night out with two girlfriends, Laura set off home by foot. She never arrived. The next evening her body was found by locals on the edge of a cricket field. She had been raped and murdered.

Here Anne tells the story in her own words:

When Laura went out at night it was usually with her boyfriend Gary. They had been going out with each other since they were seventeen, and Gary only lived a few minutes away from our house. They were inseparable, and had planned to announce their engagement in October that year.

But the night Laura disappeared she hadn't been with Gary. She had gone out with two girlfriends to celebrate one of their birthdays. They had begun the evening at a pub and had later gone on to a disco in Paisley. At around one o'clock in the morning two of the girls decided to go home because they were tired, but Laura stayed for a while longer chatting to friends. It was a beautiful summer's night and quite warm. So rather than wait at the taxi rank, where there had been quite a bit of trouble in the past weeks, Laura decided to make the short walk home.

When I got up in the morning Laura wasn't there, she hadn't gone to work nor was she with Gary. I knew instantly that something terrible had happened. Laura wasn't the type of girl to stay out all night, and even if she had, she would have called me. She was like that. So I called the police. At first they said they could do nothing because she was twenty-two and an adult. For the moment this wasn't a missing person's case. They asked us if there had been any arguments in the family or whether she had rowed with Gary. I said no. 'This isn't like Laura,' I told them calmly but firmly. 'Something has happened. She has either been abducted or murdered.' The police officers agreed they would go to the disco and see if they could find out what had happened and whether anyone knew anything or had seen Laura leave.

I will never forget that day as long as I live. It was a beautiful summer's day and very warm, but we weren't outside. My husband Archie, my son Alan, Gary and some other relations sat in our living room waiting for news.

During the day a cricket match was being played at our local cricket ground. Because of the weather quite a large crowd of spectators had come to watch the match. After the game, at about 8 p.m. a group of young people were making their way home from the match across the field. As they passed the hedgerows they spotted the body of a young woman and called the police.

The officers I had talked to about Laura, heard the news on their police radios. It wasn't long before they were standing in our house telling us that a body of a young woman had been found. She had *been murdered. Of course they couldn't confirm it was Laura then. But I knew.*

It took the police fifty-five days to find him. They said they would do DNA tests on everyone in the area if necessary. The problem was that they could find no motive for the murder. Laura was a well-liked girl and the community was shocked by what had happened. She was quiet but had a lot of friends, many of them were from her school days, others she had met at college or at work. Because Laura had worked in the local video shop nearly everyone knew her face. People were horrified.

On the night of her death, Thomas Brophy had been seen drinking at a local pub. He had made a sexual advance to a woman who had refused him. He would later testify to this in court. As Laura made her short journey home she passed the cricket field, where he pounced on her. She tried to fight back but he dragged her into the bushes where he raped her. She died from a broken neck.

Brophy was jailed for life in March 2000.

Although the trial answered a lot of questions and Brophy was prosecuted I was left with my own questions unanswered. The pathology report said that Laura would have died quickly after her neck was broken, but that wasn't enough for me. It may seem strange to some, but I wanted to know how much she had been aware of during the attack. I wanted to know how long she had been scared, whether she had been conscious while he had raped her. You cannot stop such things going through your mind. Most of all I wanted to know if she was OK now. I am a Catholic and I have always believed in an afterlife but I wanted to know, wherever she was, that she was safe and happy.

One night, lying in bed and unable to sleep I picked up a copy of

Bella *magazine. The magazine fell open on Rita's page. I had never really read her column before, but now I was drawn to it. That night I wrote to her care of the magazine and asked her if she could give me a reading. In the letter all I said was that we had lost our daughter and that I could not stop crying. That week I was called and given an appointment for a telephone reading that Sunday.*

The day of the reading came and I made sure that I was alone in the house. I took a pad and paper and went and sat in Laura's room to make the call. What happened next astounded me.

Rita began by telling me Laura's name and described her as small with long flowing hair. She said that when she died my mother Mary, who had died from cancer had met Laura, and that she had taken her by the hand and was with her. She told me that I was wearing my mother's ring and a ring that had belonged to Laura. I could not believe this. The only jewellery I was wearing that day was my mother's wedding ring and a ring Laura had been given on her sixteenth birthday.

She then said to me, 'Laura is sending you all her love and keeps saying that she is OK. But she is telling you not to cry. She knows you have cancer, she says she was there with you at the hospital'. 'Please don't cry Mum, don't cry,' were Laura's words. This information amazed me. When Laura died I had no idea I had cancer. It wasn't until December of that year that I went to the hospital to have a mammogram. I hadn't been ill. There were no symptoms. It was simply a check-up. But the doctors confirmed that I had cancer and weeks later, just before the trial, I had my breast removed. During the trial a nurse came every morning at 8.30 a.m. to change my dressings.

I was strong for the trial, but once it had ended I couldn't stop crying. The fact that I had cancer meant nothing. I didn't care if I died there and then. I had nothing to live for, I thought.

But what Rita had just told me meant that Laura was around us, she visited us, she knew what was going on, what we were going through and although that didn't bring her back to me, it was a comfort.

Rita also talked about 'Lisa'. She said that Laura liked her and wanted her brother Alan to know that. Laura never met Lisa, Alan's girlfriend. They didn't meet each other until eight weeks after Laura was buried, so again this proved to me that Laura was around.

Rita gave me the initial G and told me that he was Laura's soul-mate. She said that they had always been together and she saw him riding his bike. Gary is a fanatical cyclist. She said he was loyal, but one day he would have to move on and Laura knew this.

It was at this stage that Rita said that she could see Laura in her mind. That she was 'shining like an angel', that she was in white. At my surprise fiftieth birthday party, which had been arranged by the kids, Laura wore a white suit. It was made from a very gauzy, shimmery fabric and that night there was just something about her and the light. She looked so wonderful and people were saying, 'Look at Laura, she is shimmering like an angel.' We buried her in that suit.

Rita then said that Laura was telling her about what happened the night she died. She said to me, 'She won't say his name, it's upsetting her, she says he has been caught and that is what matters, so I am not going to press her on it.'

I wasn't calling Rita to find out who had done it. That had already been proved in court and justice had been done, but there were still some things about what happened that I wanted answers to. Things the police and the trial could not tell me.

Rita then said, 'Laura is talking about the night, she is saying to me, 'Jacket, dirty, torn.' (At this stage Rita did not know what had happened to Laura, we hadn't discussed it. All she knew was that she was dead.) On the night she died Laura was wearing a brand-new cream jacket. When she was found later it was ripped and torn and covered in mud. Rita then said, 'Greenery, bushes. I screamed and screamed.' This too fitted in with what they had said at the trial. Laura had been dragged into the bushes, and she had screamed twice. We know this because a doctor, who was in the area, told the police that he had heard a woman scream not once but twice and then heard nothing else.

Then Rita said, 'Laura keeps telling me that she was murdered and raped, murdered and raped. She is saying it in that order.' This was the information I had been waiting for. It was not only the order of the words that convinced me, but the way that Laura was repeating it. My greatest fear had been that Laura had been conscious of her attack. It was what had disturbed me the most. I had hoped that she had died or had at least been unconscious while she was raped. The police forensic scientist could only say at the trial that he was 98 per cent sure that the injury on Laura's neck would have killed her almost immediately. But I needed to be sure. I needed to know that she went quickly, that she didn't know what was happening to her, that she wasn't frightened for long. I said nothing to Rita but she carried on, 'Laura is telling me, "I stepped out of my body while he did the rape."' So, Laura had already gone. I felt relieved. Rita continued, 'She is saying to me "I could have told you who he was."' Well, as it transpired during the trial Laura could have told us who it was because she knew him. Brophy was a member of the video club where she had worked.

Rita had given me the information that I wanted and needed. But there was more. Another thing I had been concerned about was that I had wanted to know if Laura knew how much we loved and missed her. During the reading Rita said to me, 'Laura cannot believe her own funeral, she can't believe so many people turned up.' To be honest, neither could I. I knew Laura was popular and also that the community had been devastated by what had happened to this young girl, but on the day of the funeral as we made our way in the car to the cemetery I could not believe my eyes. The whole of Paisley must have turned out. Thousands and thousands of people lined the streets and I remember being so moved that as I stared out of the car window I said to myself, 'God, Laura! I hope you're looking at this. I can't believe your funeral.'

Rita's reading astounded me and gave me the answers to many questions that had bothered and upset me. It's odd, but it is the small details that gave me the most comfort. She told me that Laura was now looking after children in the afterlife. This I could well believe because she had always been a magnet to children. She loved them and they adored her. She was a natural with children. Rita also mentioned all the soft toys that Laura had – presents from Gary. She said that Laura was showing her bags and bags of shoes. Laura was a complete shoe-a-holic, it was a joke in our house. There was also a moment during the reading when Rita asked me, 'Why does Laura keep touching her nose?' And then a while later, 'She's telling me you're very nosy!' I couldn't believe that, because my children always used to say to me, 'Mum, you're dead nosy! You must be the nosiest mother in Paisley!'

To say that the reading brought me comfort would be an understatement. After the trial I was very low. But the fact that Rita told me that Laura was OK, 'I'm OK Mum, I'm OK,' she was saying, gave me the will to go on and it helped ease this terrible pain.

Rita said many other amazing things that day. Things about my mother, about a boy called Michael who had died and was the son of a colleague of mine, who Laura had met in the afterlife. There was only one thing that I couldn't understand during the reading and thought that maybe Rita had made a mistake. She kept talking about a play park. When she said it, I thought that she must think that that was where Laura had been found. And I said to her again and again, 'I think you mean a cricket ground.' 'No,' she said, 'it's definitely "play park" I'm hearing. Laura keeps going on about it.' Some time after the reading I learnt that the community, together with our local paper, the Paisley Daily Express, had set up a fund in Laura's name. They were going to build a memorial garden on some council land. But then it was decided at a meeting that because of Laura's love of children it would be more fitting if they did something else. And so they came up with a new idea – a play park.

When Rita called me recently to ask if I would mind putting Laura's story in this book, she mentioned it again. 'I was thinking of you today and I couldn't get this play park out of my head. Laura just won't let it drop today.' It was uncanny because the Laura Donnelly Play Park was opened that very week.

5. Ghosts, Poltergeists and Possessions

This may seem a little strange, given my Spiritualist beliefs, but I don't believe in ghosts. Filmy hovering apparitions, shrouded in white sheets, hell bent on causing chaos and upset are to me the stuff of horror movies and Halloween parties. That said, I do of course believe in spirits, but the notion of the ghost is just a caricature of a spirit. It is very rare for a spirit to show themselves, and when they do they certainly don't go round in white sheets with eyeholes! Nor do spirits spend time trying to spook us. When they come to us they come with love because we are unhappy, to care for us when we are down or in trouble, or they come to warn us.

When we die, as I have said before, we all become spirits. We lose and shed our physical bodies because they are no longer necessary to us, and take on a spiritual form. We all become spirit no matter who we have been in this life. As I explained in Chapter Two, the pure, the good, the godly may ascend to the highest level of the spirit world when they pass over but people who have been immoral, criminal or dangerous in this life also ascend, albeit to a lower plane.

On the whole, spirits are not something to fear. They do not come back to haunt us, to frighten us or to carry out revenge. They are at peace so there is no reason for them to bother us. My experience as a medium has taught me that spirits are there to love and protect us. Our fear of anything that is not from this world stems largely and understandably from our ignorance of the unknown. For most of us any contact with a spiritual entity is helpful.

Even spirits that are sent to the first plane of the spirit world, in other words those who have been evil in this life, cannot do anything to harm us. Once a spirit has ascended they are set on a path to spiritual purity and fulfilment, so they do not, therefore, wish us here on earth any ill intent or harm. Furthermore, as I discussed earlier, these spirits on the first plane cannot travel so they cannot come back to earth to visit us or haunt us. That said, there are some spirits who can still cause us trouble, and these are known as earthbound spirits.

In this chapter I am going to look at the different types of spirit that we may encounter in this life, looking at the visitation of the friendly spirit who we know to the more terrifying encounters with earthbound spirits.

FRIENDLY SPIRITS

Although we are visited throughout our lives by spirits, most of us remain completely oblivious of these encounters.

When spirits come to us they do so discreetly, without intrusion. It may be in the night while we are sleeping, it could be when we are driving the car, going to work or looking after our children. We remain unaware of these visits because spirits do not like to scare us or to interrupt our routines. We may not know anyone in the spirit world particularly well but that does not mean that we are not watched over and protected by our guardian angels and spirit guides. Spirits like to respect the order of things. They may miss us when they pass over but they also understand that they have to accept that for the moment they cannot be with us the whole time and they cannot live with us on this plane. For the most part they let us get on with our lives.

That said, people often write to me or contact me saying that they have had a strong sensation that they are not alone. I get a lot of letters from well-adjusted, intelligent people asking me, time and time again, whether I think that they are going mad or losing their mind. They talk of hearing footsteps or strange noises around the house. They suddenly become aware of a presence in a room. They talk of being overpowered by their loved one's smell or being awoken in the night by the sensation that the person who has passed over has been with them.

The theme of these letters is always the same. These people, no matter how educated, rational and sane, have all experienced something that defies explanation and yet to them it seems very real. A great many people dismiss these encounters as nothing more than imaginings or coincidence. They argue that the individual in these circumstances is so overcome by grief that they have lost perspective or that because they are unable to come to terms with the loss of a loved one they seek their presence in other things. They may over-interpret a coincidence, such as saying that they can smell their loved one's perfume in a room, or because of their emotional state they are irrational in believing that an electrical fault in the house has something to do with their loved one visiting them.

Cynics amongst us will always be able to come up with a

rational explanation for all of these mysterious occurrences. Yet for those who have encountered them no amount of argument can convince them otherwise. Over the years I have read for hundreds of different people, from doctors and lawyers to miners and computer experts, who have all sat in my reading room and told me similar stories, convinced that they have been in the presence of a spirit. A mother who felt her daughter hug her, a lawyer who feels her brother around her at night and claims that he changes the music she is listening to to his favourite record, a business man who heard his wife on the telephone when he was talking to another person.

The reports of these encounters are all similar to each other. People tell me how they have seen butterflies and birds at odd times, in strange situations. (In most cultures birds and butterflies are symbolic of spirit.) They tell me how after a death they have experienced problems with anything electrical – lights and computer screens flickering, televisions and radios being repeatedly switched on or off, kitchen appliances turning themselves on. In *Soul Mates* I told the story of a woman who knew that her husband came to see her because whenever she watched television at night and the snooker was on the TV would suddenly switch over. She said she knew it was her husband because it was his favourite programme and he used to do the same thing when he was alive. Of course people will argue that all these encounters can be explained in terms of power surges, breezes, climate changes, an overactive imagination and so on but to the people it has happened to, who have sat with me or talked to me, it is very real.

As I have said the majority of spirit visitations go unnoticed because spirits don't want to alarm us. But in certain situations the spirit will try and make themselves seen or heard in order to get our attention. This is either because they have a message for us or because they want to warn us about something.

Recently I did a telephone reading for a girl who said a very strange thing was happening to her and she thought she might be going a little mad. She said that even though her father had passed away a couple of years back, recently she kept smelling the smoke from his cigar.

At first she thought that she must be imagining it but as the days went on it became stronger and more pungent. She couldn't understand this because no one she knew smoked cigars, smoking was prohibited at her office and she didn't even smoke cigarettes herself.

Although she thought it was slightly irrational and mad she thought that maybe her father was trying to tell her something or send a message to her, which is why she had contacted me.

I knew none of this at the beginning of the reading but I was quick to get her father in spirit. 'Was he a cigar smoker?' I asked, having told her his name, how he had passed over and correctly telling her that she was one of four daughters. 'Yes he was!' she said.

'He is desperate to talk to you,' I said. 'He is very worried about your mum. He is frantic about her.'

As it turned out the girl was right. Her father was getting a message to her. He was worried about the way her sisters were treating her mother. The girl I was reading for was now living in Australia but she had originally come from New Zealand. Sometime after her father passed away she had moved to

Australia but she had left her mother behind in New Zealand with one of her sisters. The girl's father was telling me that this sister, who was caring for her mother, was taking her jewellery and possessions and selling them.

'Did your mother have a ruby and diamond engagement ring?' I asked her.

'Yes she did, I mean she *does*,' she told me. 'She'd never get rid of the ring, she cherishes it, it was the first thing my father ever gave her.'

'Well,' I said. 'I'm afraid she doesn't have it any more, your sister's seen to that. Your father is telling me to get to New Zealand now and sort this out. He won't rest in peace and he'll keep coming to you until it's settled,' I said to her. 'You must go soon. He is worried that she won't have anything left if your sister goes on like this, and he's being trying to get you to go for months now.'

I hadn't known about the smell of cigar smoke during the reading but when she told me later on it all made sense to me. The girl left to see her mother the following week.

In some cases I find that spirits who are desperate to contact us will actually try and show themselves in order to get our attention. In these situations you are seeing an *apparition* – in other words you are not seeing the spirit as they are now, for they no longer have that form, but a projection of how they looked here on the earth plane. They do this to prove to you that you have made contact with them, either because their message or warning is of great importance, or because they simply want you to believe that they still exist.

Although I have had many encounters with people who have seen spirits and over the years have seen a great many myself, it is, in fact, extremely unusual. Many people who come to me for readings ask whether they might be able to see their loved one again. In Chapter One I discussed how I am sometimes able to transfigurate spirits. It is very difficult to do, not only because it is physically draining for me, but also because many spirits don't like to show themselves. Moreover, transfigurations only happen when the spirit really wants to and feels the need to materialize. I can't just magic spirits out of a hat. They really have to want to come.

I call the next story my 'love story' and it is about a materialization. I have never known a couple as in love as Jenny and Andrew. They were soulmates. They did everything together, lived for each other, they were very much in love. They used to stay up at night talking and then go outside to watch the dawn break in each other's arms.

I had known Jenny for quite a while. She was a local girl who would come to me regularly for readings. Her mother had passed away and she missed her terribly. The readings with her mother were always good and clear, and she always came through. Yet there was always something that bothered me about these readings. Every time we had one I would end up asking Jenny if she drove a yellow mini. The answer was always an emphatic no. 'Rita you know I drive a Cortina,' she would say. 'I'd never own a Mini. They're far too small for me.' It was odd you see because I would get this message *every* single time we met.

Jenny had been courting Andrew, a local policeman, for a

couple of years. They were absolutely besotted with one another. One morning at around 7 a.m. I received a phone call. To be honest I had no idea who I was talking to, or what they were saying, because of the sobbing down the other end of the phone. 'Who is it?' I kept asking. 'Who am I talking to?' Eventually I realized it was Andrew.

'Bring her back, Rita. Please, bring her back!' he cried. 'It's Jenny,' he said through the sobbing. 'She was killed last night.'

'Oh God. No,' was all I could say as I sat down. 'Killed?'

'She's gone Rita. She came to fetch me from work at the end of my shift and she was killed in an accident.'

'In the Cortina?' I said.

'. . . no her Cortina was in the garage,' he said.

My heart sank. He didn't have to tell me the rest. I already knew.

Jenny's Cortina had gone to the garage. It was booked in for a couple of days, but Jenny needed a car so the garage had lent her another car – a yellow mini. Jenny had driven to the police station that night to collect Andrew at the end of his shift. She had made him a special meal and had wanted to surprise him, but on the way there she crashed. A dog had run out on to the road in front of the car. She must have swerved to avoid it. She was killed instantly. Andrew was on duty when it happened. He heard about the crash on his police radio. He heard that there had been a crash involving a yellow mini, that a young woman had been killed. He knew then that it was Jenny.

Andrew was desperate to see me that morning. He wanted to come to me straightaway. But I wasn't comfortable with this. As I said earlier I don't like reading for people too early. I like to wait until they have had the time to be accepted into spirit. At the very least I wait until they have been buried. But what could I do? Andrew was so desperate that I let him come as a friend to comfort him.

When he arrived, Mo and I were in the sitting room talking. The television was on but the volume was turned down. Andrew sat down next to me, his face swollen from crying. He was obviously completely distraught. He said nothing, just sat there staring down. Then, all of a sudden, he flung a set of keys at me. 'That's all I have left of her, that was the last thing she touched,' he sobbed. As soon as the keys hit my hands and I heard those words, I thought to myself – I shouldn't hold these! Jenny hadn't been gone long and I was scared of touching anything that had been in her possession. It was too soon for her and it was too soon for me.

I looked down at the key ring, wondering what to do next, when I saw the words printed on the round yellow fob. 'I'm on my way to heaven,' it read.

At that moment, and I have Mo as a witness for this, the room went ice cold. The TV switched off as though someone had pulled the plug and the room darkened. Andrew was silent, frozen. I turned to Mo who was staring at the corner of the room. 'She's there!' he said, signalling to the corner. Andrew and I looked over. All three of us saw her as clear as though she had just walked into the room, as though the accident had never happened.

She looked so beautiful standing there, radiant and smiling. She had been a pretty girl in life but now she looked just beautiful. The room was silent but in my head I heard her say, 'I must go now. I don't want to. I want to stay with him. But I can't. My mother is here and I have to go to her. Tell him I'll always love him.' She looked rather wistfully at Andrew and then to our amazement crossed the room, walked over to him and stroked his arm and gave him the most beautiful smile. And then she went.

I think that Jenny was able to appear to Andrew because she had not yet ascended and because he so wanted her to come. He needed to see her one last time. But I must stress here that this is extremely rare and is not something that I would as a rule recommend to anyone who has just lost someone close to them. I do believe that people should be laid to rest and given the chance to ascend into the spirit world before I try and contact them.

I find that spirits who have been in the spirit world for a while become more used to showing themselves and often when they do appear it is hard to distinguish them from people who are still on the earth plane. This is especially true of spirit children who seem for some reason to be drawn to me and quite enjoy hanging around my house!

In *From One World to Another* I told the story of Lara, a beautiful little girl who passed over when she was just four years old. Over the years Lara and I have got close and she is always around, especially when she knows that her family are about to come for a reading. I'm used to seeing her but I had always assumed that I was the only one who could see her. But a couple of years ago, when we were still at Ash House, Mo came into the sitting room from the garden and saw a blonde little girl sitting on the sofa. She was facing the other way, and he could not see her face, but Mo assumed it was Charlene, our granddaughter, who was staying with us at the time. He started chatting to her, asking how her day at school had been and if she knew where I was, when the little girl turned round and stared at him – then he realized that it wasn't Charlene after all. It was Lara!

A similar thing happened to my daughter Julie. Since the age of two my granddaughter, Ashley, who is now six, has had an imaginary friend. Now Ashley has a great deal of gypsy blood in her. Not only does she get it from me but also from her father Billie and I have always believed that she is quite 'gifted'. Ashley and her little friend have always been inseparable. When Ashley talks to her she speaks in a distinctive and grown-up manner, using long words. 'Stop being so contradictive!' [sic] she'll say to her. And yet when Ashley talks to Julie, she will speak like any other little girl of her age.

One night, not long ago, Billie and Julie stayed in and had been enjoying a takeaway in front of the television. When Julie went to the kitchen to tidy up Billie was already in bed. Before she went into the kitchen she heard a rattling of papers. She thought it was odd, given that Billie had gone straight into the bedroom when he had turned in and that Ashley had been in bed for hours. So she went into the kitchen to investigate.

Just before she turned into the kitchen she heard giggling. Ashley must be awake she thought. But when she got to the kitchen it was empty. Julie thought nothing more of it and washed the plates up but as she turned off the kitchen light and made her way down the corridor to bed, a child sped past her laughing. She thought it must be Ashley for she was around the same height and had long blonde hair – but this girl's hair was curly and Ashley's was straight.

Before she had a chance to catch up with her the girl rushed into Julie's bedroom. Julie followed her in and switched on the light, but the only person there was Billie who had fallen asleep. She crossed the corridor and went to Ashley's room but again when she put the light on there was only Ashley in a deep sleep.

I am not convinced that Ashley's friend is as imaginary as we originally thought her to be. When I was her age, as I mentioned in *From One World to Another,* I too had a little friend who turned out to be a spirit child. When I asked Ashley what her friend looked like after that night she told me that she had blonde curly hair, the same length as her own.

EARTHBOUND SPIRITS

An earthbound spirit is a spirit who has not yet ascended into the spirit world. This can happen for a number of reasons. It can be the result of an untimely death, such as a suicide or an accident (I call these Lost Spirits). Or it can be because the spirit has refused to ascend because it wants to stay here on the earth plane. This may be because it cannot bear to be parted from us – or because it feels it has unfinished business here.

As I said earlier, spirits don't set out to haunt us. Their visitations may frighten us because they are unexpected but they do not mean to upset us. Spirits may be mischievous but they do not mean any ill intent. Spirits who have ascended come only with peace and love. But I am afraid this rule does not necessarily apply to earthbound spirits.

Because they have not yet ascended and begun a journey of fulfilment and spiritual purity, earthbound spirits can be troublesome and, in some cases, dangerous, as we will see later on in this section. The majority of earthbound spirits can be exorcised from our lives and sent back to the spirit world either through prayer or by asking the spirit world to come and collect them.

Lost spirits are not harmful. Their visits can be alarming but these spirits are not evil. Often it is simply a case of them not knowing where they are, not understanding that they have passed away, and not knowing where to go. They may seem to haunt us. They carry on existing in the place that they used to live, they try and interact with us, or be with us. The majority of hauntings take place when an earthbound spirit doesn't realize it has passed away. They cannot understand why new people are living in their house and making changes, but once they have been told to leave and enter the spirit world either by a medium or priest, the trouble usually stops. In other cases where a lost spirit is causing trouble – either by making noises, playing with the electrics or even showing themselves – the spirit is asking for help.

I once read for a young woman called Lydia. Lydia was in her late twenties, worked for a bank and was happily married. She had come to me for a reading because all her life she had been haunted by something that happened to her when she was just seven years old.

Lydia's parents had moved into a new house in the Midlands. One night after having been put to bed by her mother and fallen asleep, Lydia was woken up. To her horror at the foot of the bed stood a man. He was dressed from head to foot in black but because it was dark she could not make out his face. The man didn't move and didn't say anything, he just stood there. Lydia started to scream and woke her parents who rushed into the room to see what was happening.

When they reached their daughter's room they saw no one, just their child sitting bolt up right in bed screaming. They rushed to her side to ask what was wrong but Lydia just carried on screaming and pointing at the man. Her parents could not see him, all they saw was Lydia pointing at thin air. Then all at once he disappeared.

Lydia's parents calmed her down and tried to get her to go back to sleep, assuming that this was nothing more than a nightmare. But Lydia would not go back to sleep in that room that night. In fact she never slept in that room again.

Lydia's parents never believed that there had been a man in her bedroom. To them this was nothing more than a bad dream, but Lydia was convinced of what she had seen. It wasn't a dream or a hallucination and it wasn't a shadow.

I knew nothing of this experience when Lydia came to me for a reading. The woman who sat before me in my reading room looked composed and together. It was only when the reading started that I sensed intuitively that there was something wrong.

As I spoke to Lydia, her grandmother, Phyllis, came to me. She was telling me over and over that Lydia shouldn't be scared, that there was nothing to worry about any more. As the messages came through gradually I began to get a picture of what had happened that night. I saw Lydia as a child, sleeping in her bed and then I saw her screaming. I didn't have to ask why she was frightened because I saw the spirit in my mind's eye – a dark, shadowy hulk of a man standing at the foot of her bed. I could understand why Lydia was frightened, anyone would have been, but I didn't feel that this man wanted to do her any harm. I felt as though he was lost, that he had come to her for help.

Lydia began to tell me what had happened that night, of her fear and of her subsequent frustration that no one believed her. She felt isolated because she could not discuss what had happened with her parents or her husband. And she explained that whilst she had never seen this 'man' again, she was frightened that he might return. She had come to me for a reading because she thought that I might be able to tell her who the man was and why he had come to her.

I started the reading again and began to retrace what had happened that night. I wanted to find out who this spirit was and whether he would come back to Lydia again.

As I focused my mind on Lydia I began to get a clear picture of the house she grew up in. To Lydia's amazement I described in detail the exterior of the Victorian detached family house. I saw the configuration of the downstairs rooms, the hallway, the kitchen, the sitting room and the dining room. Up a flight of stairs and down the passageway and there in my mind's eye was Lydia's room. I described the wallpaper, the curtains, the single bed positioned in the middle of the room. There was a chest covered with toys

As these images came to me I was overwhelmed by a feeling of desperation. Phyllis was telling me that the spirit meant no harm, that he wanted help. He had not meant to frighten Lydia;

he was earthbound and lost. I felt that the spirit did not have anything to do with Lydia or her family. He had come simply because he didn't understand where he was. He may not have realized that he had passed away. The reason why Lydia had seen the spirit and her parents hadn't was probably due to the fact that children are pure minded and often have far more spiritual sight than adults. By screaming, Lydia had frightened him off, and probably had sent him to the spirit world. I assured Lydia that she now had nothing to fear. I was confident that this was a one-off event and that she would not be bothered again by the spirit.

Lost spirits are easy to deal with because in most cases they want to ascend. There are some earthbound spirits who refuse to ascend because they want to remain here with the person they loved but these spirits do not usually mean any harm. I find this happens in cases of twins where one has passed away and the other hasn't, or with spirit children who don't want to be parted from their family. In these situations I try to encourage the spirit to move on, if only because they can do more good for us in spirit than they can trapped down here on the earth plane.

POLTERGEISTS AND POSSESSIONS

I said earlier that there were some earthbound spirits that we should fear and be wary of and these are the spirits that possess us, and poltergeists. Both of these earthbound spirits cannot only cause a great deal of damage, destruction, but are hell bent on terrorizing and persecuting their chosen victim.

By definition a poltergeist is an unruly, noisy and disruptive spirit. A poltergeist attack is characterized by reeking havoc around the home, from moving the odd object and piece of furniture around to literally vandalizing the place and destroying everything in its path. They never show themselves or make themselves heard, which can be even more terrifying because their victim has no idea who they are. They seem to attach themselves to people for no apparent reason and unlike a haunting seem to have no link with the house itself. In my experience they tend to target the vulnerable or the weak and statistics have shown that the majority of reported poltergeist attacks are in the 11-24 age bracket.

When I was planning this section with my assistant and thinking of what I was going to say about poltergeists, an extremely strange thing happened. We were sitting in my living room talking about how disruptive poltergeists can be when Mo came into the house. 'You won't believe what's happened outside, Rita!' he said.

'What is it?' I asked.

'It's the garden well,' he explained. 'It's just smashed to the ground. I can't understand it.'

I rushed outside and sure enough Mo was right. The wooden posts that support the roof of the well had broken, seemingly snapped in two at the base and they were lying on the lawn. It was as though the well had just keeled over. What was really odd about this was that it was a very still day, there was no wind, there hadn't been a storm, but there it lay in pieces. The wood at the base was in good condition, because it was a relatively new well, and there was no sign of rot. Whether this was a warning from a poltergeist or not I cannot say but it certainly sent a shiver down my spine and scared the living daylights out of my assistant!

As with possessions, which I shall discuss later on, poltergeists are difficult to deal with. Readings can often prove fruitless because I find that the spirits who usually protect you and communicate with me like to stay well clear of them. One reason why I am nervous about dealing with possessions, hauntings and poltergeists is because I am always terrified that the spirit will either attach itself to me, attack me because it doesn't want to be sent away or possess me. As a medium I am very sensitive to their presence and am always concerned about the repercussions of getting involved in such cases. In *From One World to Another* I told the story of how I exorcised a spirit that then latched on to me. As a result I suffered a heart attack. So to be honest I am always wary about dealing with poltergeists and possessions.

I always try to advise people who are having problems with an unwanted spiritual presence to try and exorcise the spirit themselves. Usually this can be achieved by simply chanting the mantra, 'go away and leave me alone'. However, when it comes to poltergeists I always suggest that people get as far away from the place where the attacks are occurring and hope that the poltergeist will leave of its own accord. Poltergeists are troublesome spirits, intent on terrorizing their victim. The longer you remain around the presence the more harm it will do you, so the best thing you can do is to get as far away from them as possible. The worst thing you can do is show them fear because then they know that they are succeeding and they will try to push you to breaking point.

I once read for a young woman who had serious problems

with a poltergeist. She had bought a new flat in the city. It wasn't an old building but a brand new one and she was the first occupant of the flat. She moved in and began unpacking her things but within days of trying to settle in she was having problems. It started small. Things that she was certain that she had put away, her objects, clothes and furniture started moving around the flat.

At first she thought that it must be her imagination. So far nothing very dramatic had happened. It was just that things would seem out of place. She would put a dress away only to find it on the bed. Hang a picture and find it hours later on the floor. She would unpack her books, put them on a shelf, to find them back in a packing case the next day. She began to think she was losing her mind.

But after a while it got so bad she rang me. 'I just don't know who to turn to,' she said. 'I feel like I am going mad but I know that it isn't me. I come home from work at night and things have been rearranged,' she told me. 'Every time I turn my back something moves or has been rearranged. It's not just the odd thing. Last night when I got home all my clothes had been removed from the drawers and were everywhere. I put my china away last night in a cupboard but today I find it in the sitting room.'

The woman thought she was going mad, and I think that a lot of the people she had talked to about this thought the same. But when this young woman came to me for a reading she seemed sane enough to me. She could not have been more level-headed. She worked for the Civil Service and had brought a friend with her who backed up her story. Once in the reading room I knew she wasn't lying and the reading confirmed this. I was getting a bad feeling and a warning from her grandmother in spirit. 'Whatever happens you must not go back to that place,' I told her. 'There is a poltergeist in that flat and you should stay away from it for the moment.'

I knew that there was no point in her trying to exorcise the spirit herself. She asked if I would come back with her to the flat but I was reluctant. I didn't want to take the risk. 'I don't think that it would do any good,' I said. 'The only thing you can do is to stay away from the flat for a while. Give it time and it will get bored and move on.'

The woman left Ash House and despite my warnings returned to her flat. Two days later I was woken late at night by a telephone call. I was going to ignore it and go back to sleep but when I heard her screaming into the answerphone, I had no choice but to pick it up. 'Rita please help me!' she pleaded as she told me what had happened.

That night she had returned to her flat from the office. Following her reading with me the poltergeist had left her alone. She felt confident that it had left of its own accord and she tried to get her life back to normal.

She stayed in that night and decided to make some sense of the mess in the flat and started unpacking the boxes. She was in her kitchen unpacking crockery, her pots and pans and sorting out her cutlery drawer, putting her kitchen knives into a rack when the telephone rang and she went to take the call. It was a long conversation so after she put the telephone down she decided that she would turn in for the night.

She went to her bedroom and began to get undressed when

she noticed a carving knife on her bedside table. She stared at it, trying to figure out how it had got there. She put the poltergeist to the back of her mind. Maybe she had brought the knife into the room to open the box, she reasoned. She decided not to get paranoid about it, picked up the knife and took it into the kitchen and put it back on the knife rack.

In the middle of the night she woke up feeling strange; she felt rather airy and dizzy. She turned on her bedside light and suddenly saw the carving knife on the floor by her bed. It was the very same knife she had put back on to the rack before she had gone to bed. She screamed. She knew that she had put it away. She was certain of it. At that moment to her horror the knife began to slowly rise from the floor. Frozen with fright she watched as it rose and rose until the blade was level with her chest. It then moved sideways, until it faced her, hovering in the air as it came towards her. She moved quickly, rolled off the bed and ran from the room. Still in her nightdress she fled the flat, knocked on a neighbour's door and rang her friend, who came for her. When she called me from her friend's house all I could do was comfort her. 'You're safe now,' I assured her. 'But don't go back.' I don't think I needed to give her that advice. After that night she never returned to the flat again.

Most poltergeist attacks are characterized by the moving or destruction of inanimate objects, but I once got involved with a strange case where the victims of the attack were actually physically abused.

Some years ago I was contacted by a local social worker, who asked me if I could help her with a case she had been assigned to.

The social worker had been asked to investigate a case of a woman who was allegedly interfering with her two young sons. The Social Services, having been tipped off by the woman's GP, had reason to believe that she had been interfering with her sons. There was evidence to suggest that this was the case. On examination it appeared that both boys had been physically abused. Although the boys denied that their mother had anything to do with the bruises and so forth, the finger pointed at her because, as a single mother, there was no one else in the house who could be held responsible.

The social worker could not reconcile the evidence presented to her by the authorities with the woman she had got to know and like. She was a good, doting and loving mother. She was softly spoken and had a gentle manner. She vehemently denied the allegations, but she was close to losing her children.

The woman lived alone with her sons in a dark, gloomy old house called Raven Hills. The house, which was set on the top of the hill, was remote and the nearest town was many miles away. Now, although it didn't have much of a garden, the house was surrounded by thick hedgerows of laurel. It was as though they had been planted in a ring around the house, although this was broken in parts. As soon as the social worker described the house to me and mentioned the laurel bushes I suspected that there was a problem with an unwanted spiritual presence. Laurel, you see, is a protective plant. It symbolizes purity and is supposed to ward off evil spirits. In the old days houses that were thought to be haunted were surrounded with laurel bushes to keep the spirits away. A break in the bush would signal the return of the evil spirit.

I agreed to read for the social worker to see what light I could shed on her case. At once I was being warned of the presence of an evil spirit. The boys were indeed being abused, but not by their mother but by a spirit. As I focused my mind on the family and the house, an image flashed in front of my eyes. It was the face of a man, a grotesque, hideous man, dwarf-like in stature, with twisted, gnarled features. This was the earthbound spirit that was harming the boys. This was a poltergeist who rather than reeking havoc round the house was preying on these boys instead.

I didn't want to alarm the social worker by describing what I had seen but I suggested to her that she should spend a couple of nights in the boys' room at Raven Hills to see what happened. 'That way you can see whether it is their mother or not,' I advised.

The social worker's first night in the room at Raven Hills passed without incident but she did say when she called me the next morning that she had felt airy and light-headed. The mother had not come into the room during the night and the boys seemed fine that day. But on the second night at around 12.15 p.m. the social worker, who had drifted off, was woken by screams. In the dark she managed to make out a small figure by one of the boy's beds. She thought it must be a child but when she shouted, 'Get away!' the figure turned to look at her. To her horror she saw that it wasn't a child but a hideous man. 'Tell him to stop,' screamed the boy. She went over to the bed to push him away but as soon as she moved he vanished.

Whether the social services believed the social worker's story or not I don't know but she was certainly convinced. The family were moved out of the house immediately and the case against the mother was dropped.

One of the problems with possessions is that they are difficult to diagnose. In most cases I find the victim of the possession – the host – is unaware of what has happened to them. They behave strangely, often violently, yet have no recollection of this afterwards. I think also that we tend to put a lot of possessions down to mental illness. A person starts to act out of character, so we ask if they are depressed, high or delusional. In extreme cases the person acts as though they have a split personality and so they are diagnosed as being schizophrenic. Of course I am not saying that all schizophrenics are possessions – schizophrenia is a very serious mental illness, which should always be treated by doctors – but the symptoms are incredibly similar, which is why a lot of possessions end up in psychiatric hospitals.

People who have been possessed by a spirit show signs of either having a split or multiple personality. One minute they are themselves, the next they have been taken over by the personality of the spirit, and behave completely out of character, often to the point that they are no longer recognizable in the eyes of their loved ones.

I read for a lady a long, long time ago now, who was possessed by a very evil spirit. Her husband came to see me first alone and pleaded with me to help him. He said he no longer knew the kind gentle woman he had married and that his wife had recently become prone to throwing rages in fits in which she would be violent and abusive to him or anyone around her.

Yet after these outbursts she could not remember anything

about them. He had sent her to doctors who suggested that perhaps she should see a psychiatrist or that her behaviour might be due to drink. He was at the end of his tether when he came to me. 'I just can't cope any more,' he said. 'She is beginning to think that she is possessed.'

I agreed that I would try and read her the next afternoon but to be honest I was so scared for my own safety that I left the door of the reading room open and told Mo to wait outside.

To be honest the reading didn't go at all well. I couldn't get anyone for her in spirit. To make matters worse as she sat in front of me her face kept distorting into a man's face. I knew it was the face of the spirit of the man who had possessed her but I said nothing to her husband of what I had seen, I didn't want to alarm him. After the session I apologized to her husband. 'I'm sorry but there is nothing I can do for her,' I said. 'You really should take her to a priest and see if he can help you.'

Some nights later the couple were sitting in front of the television eating their dinner. The wife had prepared some fish for their supper and everything seemed normal. Her pet cat, which she adored, was sitting on the arm of her chair and as she was eating she was feeding him little titbits from her plate. Suddenly, without any warning, the woman dropped her plate to the floor, her whole demeanour changed and without hesitation she took the fork she had in her hand and stabbed it into the cat. When her husband told her later what she had done and that she had killed her pet cat she was shocked and very upset. A priest was called to see her later that night.

What I am trying to illustrate here in the telling of this awful story is how people behave when they are possessed. It is not just a case of simply acting strangely or behaving oddly. The hosts of the possession can end up behaving extremely violently. The entity responsible for the possession won't go away until it has pushed the host to the limit and then when they have no more use for them, they set about driving you either insane or literally to your death, as this next story shows.

A man made an appointment to see me about his nineteen-year-old son who he described as being 'very troubled' and he asked if he might be able to bring him for a reading. I had read for the man before and he was a lovely man, a Buddhist with a gentle temperament. His son was an actor who had done well in his youth, acting in a Stephen King film amongst other projects. I was looking forward to meeting him.

When he walked through the door with his father and put out his hand to greet me I am afraid I stepped back. For when I saw this handsome and polite young man I could see snakes. It was as though they were coming out of his head. I could not believe what I was seeing and tried to get the vision out of my head but it wouldn't go.

The young man must have seen the expression on my face and said to me, 'Please help me, please take away the thing that has taken over me,' he pleaded. The poor boy knew that he was possessed; he was deeply conscious of the fact.

I tried to help him, and gathered my spirits and spirit guide round me to protect myself but it was no use. I was not strong enough to rid him of the demon that had taken hold of him. Every time I focused on him all I could see were these snakes curling and winding around his head. It broke my heart that I was powerless to help him, but I could do nothing.

Some weeks later his father called me to tell me that his son had thrown himself off the top of the hospital building where they were trying to treat him. He could no longer cope with the possession and so to rid himself of the evil spirit he sacrificed his own life.

Days after his death his father went to the boy's flat to collect his son's possessions. It had been a while since he had visited his son's flat but when he walked in he could not believe his eyes. Everywhere, on every inch of wall and floor were pictures his son had painted. Each one of them were self-portraits and behind his son's head, in every painting, were curling snakes.

As I discussed in Chapter One, I am against the use of ouija boards. The problem with ouija boards is not that they don't work, it's that they do. You can certainly attract a spirit by using a ouija board – the problem is the kind of spirit you are connecting with. The spirits that come forward when we are playing with these kinds of things are not from the spirit world, they are earthbound spirits. They come not because the ouija board has any spiritual pull or power (it is after all just a board no different from a Monopoly board or a chessboard), but because by sitting around and concentrating on spirits, you are inviting them to come into your world.

Unlike when I do a reading you don't know who you are communicating with. Spirits in the spirit world don't lie, so when a person comes to me and says they are your grandmother, then they are. Moreover, even if they are the lowest plane in spirit the spirit I am connecting with can't do you or me any harm because they have ascended. But when you are playing with the ouija board you never know who you are talking to.

I find that earthbound spirits are great mind-readers. When you sit down in front of a ouija board the likelihood is that you are immediately thinking of a person on the other side who you have known. You think to yourself 'Mary'. The earthbound spirit will pick up on this through ESP and will then spell out their name. You assume once the name has been spelt out that you have made contact with them but you haven't. The earthbound spirit is impersonating them. Unlike a reading you have no way of checking that you have the right person in spirit. You are not getting the details that a medium would receive in a reading such as names, places, ages and so forth. What you are doing here really is asking for trouble.

I have brought this up here because over the years I have seen a great many young people who have suffered from possessions and what links these people together is that they have all at some stage in their lives used a ouija board.

Young people love ouija boards. Calling up the dead is a rite of passage for most teenagers. They see it as nothing more than a bit of fun and are thrilled and excited by the horror stories, but I am afraid that not all the stories are just stuff and nonsense. As I have witnessed over the years, many turn out to be true.

Research has shown that the highest incidence of possession occurs amongst the 12–19 age group. In my opinion this is because people of that age are incredibly vulnerable and impressionable, and are attractive to wayward spirits.

A couple of years ago I was visited by a man who said that he needed my help urgently. There was something wrong with his teenage daughter. When he arrived at my house he could not stop crying, he was desperate, full of despair. When I read for him, I discovered that his daughter, a good-natured girl of fifteen, was causing havoc. She had, as he told me later, 'gone off the rails'.

It had started small. She started going out at night against her parents' wishes and not coming home until the early hours of the morning. She then started throwing bricks through people's windows and damaging people's property. At first her parents put this behaviour down to growing up and tried to discipline her. One night following an argument with her mother, she hit her across the face with a baseball bat. It killed her.

She was sectioned after that. The doctors believed that this horrendous act sprung from schizophrenia. She spent periods in hospital being monitored and examined by a team of psychiatrists. During these investigations it transpired that a couple of weeks before the dramatic change in her personality she had practised the ouija board with a group of friends. She had thought it was nothing more than a harmless game. How wrong she was. Their fascination with the ouija board became more than a passing interest. They played it as often as possible for a number of weeks. Around that time the girl's behaviour underwent a severe change.

Her father begged me to see her. He couldn't cope any more. She didn't, he explained, know why she was in hospital. During those moments he was with his daughter, she would ask him, 'Why have you put me here Daddy? What have I done wrong?' She genuinely had no idea what she had done. She had no recollection of the havoc she had caused, nor any memory of her mother's death.

Seeing his despair, but with reluctance, I agreed to meet his daughter with a view to finding out who had possessed her and with any luck exorcising them from her body. I insisted, however, that she came to me with two male nurses to protect myself in case she lashed out at me.

When he arrived with his daughter I knew there was nothing I could do to help. She walked up the driveway looking like any pretty fifteen-year-old but as soon as she set eyes on me and was led into my reading room she flipped. She flew into such a violent rage and temper, screaming and shouting that even the nurses had problems restraining her. I thought she might kill me. She was taken away back to the hospital and as far as I am aware is still there. By playing with the ouija board this poor girl had effectively invited a spirit to possess her. I can only hope and pray that one day it will leave her.

6. Hauntings and Houses

In this chapter I want to try and move away from the stereo-typical image of the haunted house as some old creaky mansion perched on the top of the hill occupied by a headless ghost who stalks the corridors every night at the stroke of midnight. Hauntings are seldom like this and what's more they can happen to any of us, at any time, wherever we live. A haunting is just as likely to happen, for instance, in a brand new semi-detached house in a leafy close in the suburbs as it is in some rambling old castle in Scotland. Whilst the castle in Scotland has more of a history of owners and tenants than the brand new semi, remember that the land that the semi was built on has a history too.

The bricks and mortar of a building and the ground where the foundations of a house are laid, soak up and absorb the atmosphere and history of its former occupants. Houses and the land that they are built on are the stages where the domestic dramas of our daily lives are played out. They are the settings for our childhoods, marriages, love affairs, break ups and our deaths so it isn't therefore surprising that they pick up the vibrations of our lives and attract spirits.

This is one of the reasons why Romany gypsies burnt their caravans when they passed over. In Romany culture it was traditional for the person who had passed away to be placed in their caravan with their possessions and for it to be set alight. The dead man or woman would take what was needed with them into the next world and the idea was that they left nothing behind. Whilst I am by no means advocating this practice as a way of avoiding hauntings and unwanted spiritual presences, I do think that sometimes we should be aware of the history of the place we are thinking of moving to before we settle there.

My experiences at my house at Doe Lea, which I wrote about in *From One World to Another*, are undoubtedly responsible for the way I look at houses now. From the moment I set eyes on that house I knew that there was something wrong about it. Crossing the threshold I was overcome with a sense of unease that wouldn't leave me until the day we moved out. This was my first proper family home. It was spacious, well equipped and even had a proper bathroom suite and running water, which back then was something of a luxury, to say the least! Despite my efforts to transform it into a family home, no amount of redecoration, pride or airing could remove the sense of foreboding that hung over that property. In retrospect the strange noises at night, the infestations of cockroaches, the eeriness of the hallway and the repugnant sickly sweet smell that lingered in every room should have been signs to me to get away from the house as soon as I could. But I did not read the warnings. I was young, still unsure of my gift, and didn't want to offend my first husband who had worked so hard to get us the house. In the end my initial instincts were proved right and it wasn't long before we were literally driven out by an unwanted, vicious and terrifying earthbound spirit.

Hauntings come in many shapes and forms. It is not simply a question of things going bump in the night or coming face to face with a ghostly apparition. In the majority of cases that I come across the occupants of the haunted house tell me that they just feel that there is something not quite right about the place from the moment they cross the threshold. They may simply feel uncomfortable there without ever really knowing why. Strange noises late at night, problems with the electrics, sudden darkness in a well-lit room, lingering odours and draughts in a well-insulated house – all these can be symptomatic of a haunting. By a haunting I am not necessarily talking about a house filled with spooks and ghouls but a house occupied by a spiritual presence.

Recently I got a letter from a couple who sold their house against the wife's instincts. She didn't want to leave the house but she could not explain why. There was something inside her saying don't do it but she couldn't articulate her fears to her husband so eventually she gave in and agreed to sell it.

When they moved to their new house the wife still did not feel happy. She 'grieved' for her old home and felt uncomfortable in her new one. 'I feel overwhelmed and confused here,' she said in a letter she wrote to me nine months after the move. She couldn't explain the way she felt. She knew it wasn't logical. 'Is this house wrong for us?' she asked me in her letter. 'Or am I just imagining it?'

During her telephone reading the woman's father came through. He was a great man with a lovely sense of humour and was giving me much information about the woman's family. He knew that she wasn't happy in the house. He said that it did not welcome her but he wanted her to hang on in there for a while because he knew that she would move again very soon. She listened to what I said, stayed put and later wrote to say that out of the blue her husband's job had posted them to a new area where they had a new wonderful home and she felt happy again.

Houses can be wrong for people, in the way that some people can be wrong for each other. A house that looks wonderful, has great space, an enviable view and a perfect location, in short an estate agent's dream, may not make you feel as happy as your old house which may have been cramped, falling apart, on the wrong side of town and so forth.

Often when this happens to us we are at a loss to explain why. We may feel that we are being irrational, illogical, we may even feel as though we are going mad. However my advice to you would be to follow your instincts. In the next chapter I am going to talk about how spirits and your guardian angels send you these feelings for a reason but for now it's enough to say that these feelings are a warning. Your own spirits and guardians are telling you that this house isn't right for you. It may not be haunted but they are telling you that in this house you will not be happy or something bad might happen. Or that if you stay here something will go wrong. It may not be sinister. It could just be that you would be better off in another place. The woman in this last reading had this sensation; she felt this in her unease at leaving her old house. Fortunately, she was going to move soon and I felt that this new place was right for her.

Not all 'hauntings' are bad. Sometimes we confuse a visitation from a friendly spirit with that of an evil earthbound one who is out to cause us upset and harm.

I had a letter from a woman asking for help because since

moving to her new home her five-year-old son had been seeing visions in the middle of the night and was obviously petrified. On five occasions the little boy had seen something that had terrified him, so much so he couldn't speak. When these incidents occurred he would just stand frozen and scream and scream. Afterwards he would not let go of his mother. His mother had eventually come to the conclusion that their house was haunted.

Questioned by his parents about these incidents the child claimed that he saw a man. Often he would see the man standing by his baby sister's cot. Sometimes he would be standing at the window when the boy was playing outside. The family were so frightened for the boy and for themselves, and the situation had got so out of hand that they eventually called on their local priest for help. He came to the house and blessed it and them. For a week or so after the priest's visit everything quietened down. But then it started all over again. It was now so bad that when the family went out during the day and returned to the house, the boy would have a tantrum and refuse to go back into it. After a while they put the house on the market, but it just wouldn't sell.

The woman had asked me if I thought that her house was haunted. I couldn't be sure so I gave her a reading to see what if anything was going on there. During the reading the woman's grandmother came to me in spirit and told me her name. She sent her love to the family and told me a bit about them all. Another elderly woman came through and gave her name to me and said that she was there with her son John. I liked John very much in the reading. He was warm, friendly and mild mannered so I was a bit taken aback when he told me that he was the family's 'visitor', that he had been the one who had been 'haunting' their house. John explained to me that there had once been a family feud, long before his own death, and he had fallen out with the woman's mother while he was caring for his own mother. Feeling that he had been in the wrong and caused a lot of trouble, and in an effort to make it up to the family, he had been visiting their house and had been looking after the children.

He had been with them a lot: standing over the baby's cot to make sure she was OK and at one stage closing a window because he thought she might be cold. He said that he watched the boy from the window as he played to make sure he was safe. He was sorry that he frightened them all and hadn't meant for the boy to see him. He said he would be more careful in future and promised not to scare anyone.

As I explained to the woman in this reading there was nothing wrong with the house itself. It wasn't haunted so there was no need to put it back on the market. The fact that it hadn't sold had more to do with the property market than any spook. That said there was no denying that there was a spiritual presence in the house. Anyone who has lost people dear to them are visited by spirits during the day and night – the difference is that we don't usually know that they are around. We can't see them so they don't bother us. The problem here was that the spirit was showing himself to the boy, which was obviously terrifying for the child. I can't be sure why this happened but one explanation for this is that children are less spiritually blind and deaf than adults, because they are less cynical, sceptical and are more pure. As it happens the boy never did see John's spirit again. Either he was being more careful or he stopped visiting.

*

Confusing a visitation with a haunting is an easy mistake to make. Hauntings are rare and only occur when either something bad has happened in the property or when there is an earthbound spirit around you. Most visitations – although in some cases these can be just as alarming – are in fact from friendly spirits. Recently I had a letter from a woman who said she was frightened and couldn't sleep at night, because on a couple of occasions she had been woken by the sound of footsteps only to find when she had switched on the light that there was no one there. On another occasion she felt that there was someone sitting at the end of her bed. She wrote to me to ask whether I thought she was being haunted and if so who was it?

This wasn't a haunting but spirits coming to her in the night to bring her love and protect her and her little boy. When I read for her I discovered that it was her grandparents who were coming to her at night. They hadn't meant to scare her but wanted just to be with her.

In normal circumstances the woman would not have been able to hear them or feel their presence in her bedroom. They would have been there but she would not have noticed. However, I got the feeling that the woman was psychic herself. When her grandmother came to me in reading she mentioned bells. She was saying that she rang them out when her husband arrived in the spirit world because she was so glad to be reunited with him. When I asked the woman if that meant anything to her she said it did.

She told me that when her grandfather had died she heard bells ringing. It was the middle of the night, but it was not on the hour, she did not live near a church and she could not recollect ever hearing the bells before. The next morning she found out that her grandfather had passed away at the exact same time she heard the bells. She had been scared at the time but now felt touched that her grandparents were around and protecting her and her family. In future when she heard footsteps I am sure she would be relieved and happy.

Although houses don't have souls as such they are stamped with the people who live there and who have lived there in the past. Whilst I would have no reservations about moving near a grave-yard I would be wary about moving to a house where you know something bad has happened – only because there is the possi-bility that there could be an earthbound spirit there. Which is what happened to me at Doe Lea.

One piece of advice I can give is that if you are unsure about your house and think that it might be haunted then you should check out its history. You could do this either by asking neigh-bours about the previous occupants, or by going to the local library and finding out about your local area or your house itself. If your house is new and you are having problems then look and see what stood in its place before, or if there was a building with a history near by that has since been torn down. In the majority of cases once you know what the problem is you can get rid of the spirit simply by asking it to leave.

I got a call from a woman called Jane who was having problems with her house. She was convinced it was bringing her bad luck. One bedroom in particular she said had never 'felt right'. Guests who had used it complained that they had not been able to sleep there even though the spare beds were brand new. All their attempts to sell the house had failed. She said that she felt as though the house would not let them go, as though it was keeping them there even though they didn't want to be there any more.

The crackling line during our conversation on the telephone convinced me that she did indeed have a serious problem. And this wasn't a problem with the exchange either. I can always detect a spiritual presence from interference on the telephone. It can sound a bit like a crossed line – the only difference being that the person on the other end of the telephone cannot hear the voices that I am hearing, just the crackle.

During this reading I was getting a clear picture in my mind of a young man. He couldn't have been more than twenty-one and he was a nice-looking boy. I wasn't communicating with him because he wasn't on the spirit plane. I could just see him in my mind's eye. This picture would have been sent to me by my spirit guide who was also giving me his name. My spirit guide was telling me that the boy had taken his own life. His heart had been broken so he had thrown himself from a third-floor window. The room had been his bedroom.

I passed on the information to Jane. 'Is the room on the third floor?' I asked.

'Yes it is,' she said.

'Does it look out on to a lawn?'

'Yes.'

'Is there a paved area just outside the house?' I continued.

'Yes.'

I proceeded to describe the room as I saw it in my mind; the sash window, the chair rail, the cornice. 'That's it!' she said. 'That is the room where the problem is.'

'This spirit doesn't mean you any harm,' I told her. 'But he is there, he has lost his way and needs to be sent to the spirit world. Until that happens you will have problems because he is trying to find his way, which is why he is disturbing you.'

I explained to Jane that the reason why this boy was earthbound was probably because he had taken his own life. Because his death had been untimely no one had been to collect him. I felt that had he not taken his own life he might still be alive, which is why he hadn't been collected – the spirit world weren't ready for his arrival. Feeling lost he may have attached himself to the family, which is why he didn't want them to leave and why he was preventing the sale of their house. I instructed Jane to return to the room and ask him to leave. I thought that she would be able to do this on her own because he wasn't a bad spirit and because I thought that he would want to leave and enter the spirit world anyway.

Jane did this the following day. A few weeks later Jane called to say that the problems had stopped. The room felt airy again and she felt comfortable in there. She also said that she had been doing some research into the history of the house. When she talked to her neighbours she had discovered that about twenty years earlier a young boy had lived at the house with his family but following a bout of depression he had committed suicide – by throwing himself from his bedroom window.

Spirits who are earthbound do get attached to the house that they are in and they don't like disruption or change. I often find that this is why spirits get active when a house goes on the market. They may have been giving you a hard time but from their point of view better the devil you know! Another thing that they don't seem to like is change in the house. I am not talking about the odd spot of redecoration but restructuring of the property – they don't like rooms being moved or changed or anything that throws their bearings. I have always had a lot of spirits around me because of what I do and I find that builders and painters can't do a job quick enough in my house. Strange things have happened when I have had work done. Ladders have fallen, tools have gone missing, doors to rooms that need work have been mysteriously locked. I must be the luckiest woman in the British Isles because when builders come to my house they just don't do the job on time they do it as fast as they possibly can!

Be very careful in your house if you are going to alter anything and again it might be worth doing a little detective work about the history of the house before you do anything too drastic. I knew a lady once who told me that she was going to open up her cellar at the bottom of her house. 'It's going to be wonderful,' she beamed at me, 'think of all that extra space!'

Without wanting to alarm her or to ruin her home improvement plans I said, 'Don't do it! Don't whatever you do touch that cellar.' I was getting a strong warning in my head for her not to do it. She just looked at me, slightly taken aback, raised an eyebrow and gave me one of those smiles that said either you are off your head or you're just jealous! So she went ahead and opened up her cellar, a cellar that had been cemented over by the previous owner for a very good reason. She opened up the cellar and she let out a spirit. Suddenly her house was freezing cold and dark, there was a foul stench about the place and objects moved and broke. She was forced to move out a week later. Whoever it was down there had no intention of sharing the house with her.

Just as spirits can attach themselves to properties they can also attach themselves to objects. This is particularly true of jewellery, as I have mentioned, but spirits can also forge relationships with pieces of furniture too. Like my Romany ancestors I do believe that you should be careful when you pass on or inherit possessions. As with houses, ask yourself what the history of this brooch, ring, bureaux, wardrobe is before you bring it in to your life. As this next story shows objects can actually bring an unwanted spiritual presence into a house which isn't actually haunted. This story is told by Helen, my hairdresser and friend.

My mother had been trying to sell her bungalow for a while. One Sunday afternoon while my husband Mark and I were visiting her, a car drew up down the driveway. Naturally we all got up to see who it was. Much to our surprise and to hers, it was Rita who got out of the car. She had been looking for a house in the area and had been sent the details of my mother's place. In fact the bungalow, for a number of reasons, wasn't right for Rita but she came in anyway and we all had a cup of tea.

A couple of days later when I was talking to Rita on the telephone she suddenly said to me, 'I had bad vibes about your mother's house.' I asked her what she meant and she said, 'I'm not sure but there was a bad feeling there.' And then quite out of the blue she said, 'It has something to do with a chair. Is there an old chair in the house?'

Now during the visit Rita hadn't really been round the house. I don't think she had gone further than the sitting room because she already knew that the house wasn't for her. But sure enough in my mother's dining room was an old chair. It had belonged to my father who had inherited it from his Uncle Bill. Bill was quite a reclusive man and had kept the chair in his house until he died. We called it the monk's chair because it had originally come from Chap Abbey in the Lake District.

When my father left my mother she hadn't known what to do with the chair. She tried to return it to him but ended up hanging on to it. I assumed that Rita must be referring to the monk's chair during our conversation but was taken aback by what she said next. 'Tell your mother she must get rid of that chair, it's causing her problems. It has a spirit attached to it and it must be got rid of.'

Rita mentioned my father's uncle, she said his name was Bill and then to my surprise asked, 'Was he a reclusive man?' I said yes, stunned by the information she was giving me. 'But it didn't come from him originally, did it?' she said. 'It came from an abbey. I can see the face of a monk and he is telling me it's his chair. He is the spirit who is attached to it'.

There was no question in my mind. It must be the chair. How could Rita know all of this? I told my mother about this. She said that she had been planning to get rid of the chair anyway when she moved so I urged her to do it straightaway. But the day she was going to take it off to be sold she had a change of heart.

That night when she was sleeping she was awoken suddenly by the most enormous pressure on her. She said it was as though someone was sitting on top of her and she could not move. She was very frightened. She lay there for what seemed like ages until finally she must have drifted off. The next morning she went and sold it.

Within days of the chair going my mother commented on how

she felt like a weight had been lifted from her, that her strange feeling had gone, also on how the house seemed to be much brighter. She had complained in the months leading up to the sale of the chair on how dark the house would get even if the lights were on. Within a month the house was sold.

I doubt very much that the spirit of the monk wanted to harm Helen's mother but he was causing her terrible problems. It may have been that he didn't want her to leave the house but nevertheless it was an unwanted presence. The presence was oppressive which is why Helen's mother kept feeling strange and why the house had a bad vibe about it. The fact that she was seeing darkness even when all the lights were on is another indication of a spiritual presence.

Spirits can get very attached to their possessions. Although they no longer need them when they ascend, I do find from time to time in my readings that spirits get very upset when they feel that something that once belonged to them is in the wrong person's hands. You should never meddle with a will or take something from the person who had died if it was intended for someone else. If you do you are really asking for trouble! I find that objects and jewellery that are meant for us, but have been taken by another person, do come back to us eventually. Spirits like to make sure we have what is rightfully ours and I find that they will often intervene and get back what was taken from us.

A while back I had a friend called June who lived near the sea. June was one of those people who everyone turns to when they are in trouble. She had a big heart and could never say 'no' to anyone. Her house was always filled to the brim with waifs and strays, the sick, the old and the miserable. I don't know what it was about her, she was just a magnet for people in trouble.

June lived alone with her seventeen-year-old daughter Ursula. Now Ursula was a lovely girl, she was humorous, had a good mind and had the most angelic face you have ever seen. But poor Ursula was also in a wheelchair – not that *she* ever complained about it. She was seriously physically disabled.

June and Ursula live in a terraced house on the promenade next to an elderly man called Tom. June took care of a lot of the elderly in the area but she was particularly fond of Tom, who despite being a cranky old thing was good company, and anyway she had known him for years. So when things got too much for Tom, and it got difficult for June to care for both him and Ursula, she suggested that he move in with her, just till he found his feet again and his health improved.

The months went by but Tom didn't get any better. He just got worse and one morning when June went to stir Tom and give him his tea she couldn't wake him up. He had gone.

The trouble didn't start till the spring. Around that time June decided that she would clear the house and rearrange it. One night she was woken by Ursula's screams. She rushed to her side and tried to calm her. But Ursula was inconsolable. She claimed that she had felt someone in her bed, she said she had felt something under the sheets, that the bed had banged up and down. It happened several times. It got so bad that Ursula said the bed banged up and down so hard she thought she was going to fall out, and the lamp shade on the overhead light whizzed round and round. If this was not all terrifying enough, poor

Ursula couldn't run from the room; she couldn't move from her bed without June's help.

'I don't know,' said June when she popped round to my house. 'Ursula's a good girl, but I can't help thinking that she has imagined it all. Maybe it's her hormones,' she said.

Now I knew Ursula and liked her very much. I knew she had her problems, especially being in a wheelchair, but I also knew she wasn't the kind of girl to make things up or start imagining things. She had a good head on her shoulders that girl. So when June asked me if I would go to the house I agreed. June didn't think that the house was haunted. She wanted me to visit to find out what was wrong with her daughter.

As soon as I got there I knew what the problem was. 'It's him!' I said.

'Who's "him"?' asked June.

'Tom! He's been here.' As I started to read June I could see him. He was materializing his image right behind her.

'He's looking for something,' I said.

'What is it?' June said, lowering herself into an armchair.

'Money,' I replied.

'But he hasn't got any money. He never had a penny. Why do you think that I took him in?'

'Oh he had money all right June,' I laughed. 'And lots of it too.'

Tom was a devious old thing. Likeable, but devious. Tom had money. He had thousands of pounds which fifteen years ago could have got him all the care and help he needed. But he liked June; he liked her company, and why pay for all that when you've got it next door for free. I felt that Tom was coming back for his money because not only was he tight but he didn't trust a soul with it either.

'June,' I said. 'You've moved Ursula, haven't you? You've moved her out of her room and put her in to Tom's.'

'Well, yes, I have,' she said, looking flustered. 'It's a much bigger room and I felt that Ursula needed more space.'

'It's in the room,' I said.

'What is?' she asked.

'The money! Tom's hidden the money in the room. It's under her bed. That's what he's looking for, that's why he's been near her bed. He's not trying to interfere with her, or frighten her, he just wants to get his money out from under the bed. Go and look!' I said. 'I'll bet you I'm right.'

June went upstairs and following my instructions moved the bed and rolled away the carpet, which she noticed was loose anyway. She took a crowbar to the floorboards and lo and behold guess what she found: a box with three thousand pounds in it!

It's likely that Tom wasn't trying to get the money for himself. He after all had no use for it and it may well be that he wanted to alert June to its whereabouts. June said that she wouldn't keep the money but with Tom having no family and she being his only friend and carer it was decided that she should take it. After that there was no trouble so I guess Tom was happy that June had it. Perhaps that's what he had intended all along.

Just as we have bad feelings about houses we can also have good ones. I think that our relationship with where we live can be as important as the relationship that we have with other people in our lives. Having a bad feeling about where you live can be as upsetting as having a bad feeling about someone close to you. You should always feel comfortable in the place that you choose to make your home. Trust your instincts as to whether that place is right for you or not.

Perhaps it has something to do with my Romany blood but I have always moved around a great deal. Following my marriage to my first husband Dennis we seemed to be constantly moving from one house to the next, which with four young daughters was no easy feat. Some years after Dennis had passed over and I had got together with Mo I suddenly had this strong urge to settle. We had been living at the time in a house in Clipstone, just outside Mansfield. I'm not sure why, because our house was actually perfectly nice, but while we were there I suddenly felt the compulsion to move. I think that I was searching for somewhere where I felt that I belonged. I never felt that our house at Clipstone was really home.

In fact it was Mo who found Ash House for us. He had been reading the local paper one day when he saw an advertisement – 'large house for sale with an acre of land'. For one reason and another the owner was looking for a quick sale. The house was falling apart around her and it was beginning to make her feel uneasy. When we met her she said that she and her husband had experienced a number of supernatural experiences there. She believed that the house was full of spirits.

Ash House may not have been everyone's idea of the perfect home. Set on a hill against the backdrop of the Derbyshire moors, it was an austere, imposing Victorian house, which needed a great deal of work. None of this meant anything to me.

I was already drawn to that house. Even without seeing a picture of it I knew that I should live there.

As a child my Romany grandmother had made five predictions about my life. She told me I would marry young and that I would have four daughters, and that the first three would all be born on the same numerical day of the month. She said I would learn to use my gift and one day become famous because of my work. And she also said that I would be a house dweller. 'One day, Rette,' she said to me, 'you will live in a large house with a chapel.' As all of my grandmother's predictions had so far come true I had no reason to question the inevitability of this one!

So there I was on the telephone to the owner of Ash House arranging a time to view the property, when I found myself saying, 'Look, I know this might sound a bit strange to you, but can you tell me: is the house next to a chapel?'

She paused. 'Well, yes it is,' she said. 'As a matter of fact it's next to an old Methodist Chapel. But how did you know?'

I think that you are meant to have houses and houses are meant to have you – in the way that we are meant for one another. Just as houses belong to you, you belong to them. When I visited Ash House the next day, I discovered that the owner hadn't oversold it to us on the phone. It was uninviting, cold and dark. It needed work done on it and money thrown at it, but to me I was home, I felt I belonged there. We took it there and then, without even getting further than the hallway.

For a long time we were very happy in that house. We filled it with animals, made something of the garden and loved being there. It may sound odd but as soon as I moved in, this once dark house seemed to brighten as if to welcome me. The house was filled with spirits, some of these moved here with me, others came with the house! But none of them were sinister – they were mostly spirit children.

Mo and I stayed at Ash House for thirteen years. To be honest I should have moved after twelve, the last year there was hard on me – and thirteen has never been a good number for me. I think that it's possible to grow out of and grow away from a house.

My health had meant that I could no longer manage such a large house. I couldn't get up and down the stairs and it just seemed such a waste to be using one floor. There was another reason for our move. Around this time there had been a great deal of publicity about the fact that I read for the Princess of Wales. It was prompted by a visit that she made to me with Dodi Fayed shortly before she passed over. When the media got wind of this they sieged my home, camping outside the gates hoping that if the sum was right I might spill the beans on her private life. Of course this was and still is something that I would never do but they were relentless. A mob of hundreds of journalists and photographers from around the world would not get the message and go away and leave us in peace.

I think that the Princess had been upset about what had happened to me. She felt responsible and knew that it was making me very depressed. Mo and I had already decided to move to a bungalow but we were having real problems selling the house and finding a new one in the area.

'I can see you in a bungalow,' she would muse on the telephone with me late at night. 'A house with a little land, off the road so you get some privacy, a pool for your health and a beautiful view.'

For months and months I looked for the perfect place but with no joy. I wanted to be in the area so that I could be close to my family but there was nothing. Fed up by the intrusion of the press I eventually moved to my holiday home in Skegness, the press moved on and after a while we sold our house. I had given up hope of ever finding the place I dreamed of and so had decided that for the moment I would settle in Skegness. We went back to Ash House to pack it up, leaving what we didn't need behind, but I did take the disabled bath the Princess had bought for me. The day we were packing an envelope came through the door. It hadn't come in the post and it was addressed to me, but I had no idea who had delivered it. I still don't.

Inside was a piece of paper with details of a bungalow. There was no photograph but just as I knew with Ash House, I knew that this house would be my home. We made an appointment to view it that afternoon and again as soon as I had crossed the threshold I felt like I had come home. 'I'll take it!' I said without even looking around. The owner of the property seemed a little surprised but said to me, 'Well, I hope you like marble.'

'I do but why?' I asked.

'Because the house is full of it,' he said. The owner explained that his family were marble cutters and it was true the house was full of this wonderful stone. I asked if I could see the bathroom. It was the only room I wanted to look at because I needed to see whether my special bath would fit in it. He led me through the master bedroom into the bathroom, which was certainly big enough for my bath. It was decked out in marble from floor to ceiling. 'It's beautiful!' I said.

'It should be,' he replied. 'You know this is the same marble we used on Princess Diana's bathroom at Kensington Palace!'

So here I am living in the house I had dreamed of and had seen in my mind's eye. It's a bungalow, with a little land, off the road so I get some privacy, it has a wonderful view and a heated pool. Just like she said.

7. Into the Future

People often ask me how I am able to foresee and predict future events. They want to know how I am able to tell them that there is going to be a car crash, for example, or that a windfall of cash is about to come their way. To be brutally honest about this – I can't see into the future. I can't predict what will happen to you in life. I have no idea when or who you are going to marry, if you will be rich and happy or whether your father will eventually get better. I can't predict the future but what I can do, as a medium, is to tell you what your spirits are predicting for you. I am only a channel through which these prophecies are relayed and what I tell you about your future comes not from my own insights but from the spirit world.

The reason why spirits are able to predict what is going to happen to you in the future is that from the moment we are conceived and our soul enters us, our lives are fated and have been mapped out for us. Each of our lives is predestined to follow a certain course. The major events of our lives, such as our births, marriages, deaths, have already been determined by a greater force.

Many people find the concept of destiny alarming because it implies that we, as humans, have no free will. If our lives have already been mapped out for us then we have no choice, no freedom of action, no ability or power to change the course of our lives. To all intents and purposes we are nothing more than puppets fulfilling a role, playing out lives that have already been chosen and decided by a greater force. What is the point of even trying to make a difference to our lives when we are powerless to do so, people argue?

The point to stress here is that predestination does not affect every aspect of our lives – it only serves as a blueprint for the main significant events. It is similar to making a journey. You are destined to arrive at a certain place but like any trip there are a number of different routes you can take to arrive at that particular destination. It is up to you to choose the route that you want to take. Sometimes the path that we choose may not be the best one, we may get lost, or take a longer, more complicated route than we should have done. At other times our journey may take us no time at all, and we confront no setbacks.

You may be destined to meet your soulmate and spend the rest of your lives together, for example, but it could be that it takes you a while to find them. You may have to go through a couple of relationships before you find the one, and it is these other relationships that lead you eventually to your soulmate. Ultimately, you will find your soulmate if that is what has been destined for you, but the route you take to meet them is up to you.

Predestination allows the medium to pass on prophecies from the spirit world to you – prophecies that should make your life easier and your journey more comfortable.

The ability to relay messages that relate to the future is called futurizing. Through futurizing the medium can forecast events that will happen to you at some time in your life. This could be a forthcoming relationship, a problem at work, a death in your family or a birth. The medium is only able to tell you this information because they are being told of what lies ahead by their guides. It is not up to the medium to predict future events and would be wrong for them to do so, as mediums don't have that power, gift or foresight. Anything they said that did not come directly from the spirit world would be only speculative.

I would say that 70 per cent of people who consult mediums on a *regular* basis do so in the hope that they will get answers about what will happen to them in the future. They want to know if they are going to be happy, rich, successful or find a soulmate.

Of course, futurizing can help with this. In a reading spirits may reassure you with news about your future in order to stop you from worrying or help you realize what you want from life by giving you a push in the right direction. But futurizing isn't just about telling fortunes. Being able to receive images and messages from the spirit world that relate to future events can help save lives.

Spirits cannot tell you anything that is going to interfere with your fate line. If you are destined to die at a certain time then they cannot stop this from happening. I am often asked by people why mediums can't do more to protect people. The fact is we are only told of accidents and deaths if they are not supposed to happen. If a person comes to me wanting to know when, where and how they are going to die it is extremely unlikely that I am going to be able to give them an answer. If I don't foresee a death, or an accident, then that is because I am not supposed to. I am not told about it or warned of it because that is your destiny, that is your fate. A spirit, through me, can warn you of an avoidable accident but they do so only because that is not your fate. I can tell you not to do something, not to travel in a car on a certain day, to be wary of an individual or to go and have a check-up at your doctor's, but only because this is not how you are destined to go. Of course, all I can do is pass this warning on to you – it is up to you to decide whether or not to pay any attention to this advice. I can't prevent the accident from happening, I can't force you to see the doctor, or not to let the stranger in your house. Once you leave my reading room the path you choose to take is up to you. I am only the messenger. I am not God.

As I keep saying spirits are here to protect us so they will go out of their way to stop bad things from happening to you. You don't need to be in regular communication with a medium for this to happen. Often a spirit will intervene to stop you from coming to harm. This might be as simple as moving your keys, so that you can't find them, preventing you from leaving the house at a certain time. As you search for them you think to yourself, 'But I know I left them there on the table!' You probably did leave them on the table, but the spirit has moved them. The time you spend searching for your keys is the time the spirit needed to give you to stop you coming to harm.

Spirits are around us all the time watching over us and trying to protect us. I believe that they intervene more often than we think in order to keep us from events they foresee. They may delay our plans just to keep us away from danger. Sometimes that split second is, after all, all we need to protect us. In other cases spiritual intervention can be more dramatic.

Last summer I threw a small party at my home for my children, grandchildren and friends. We were having drinks and a buffet lunch in the games room at my house and I had said to the children to bring their friends along. My youngest daughter Kerry had invited her friend Vicky over for the day. Now at that stage I didn't know Vicky very well, I had seen her a couple of times but I hadn't spoken to her. She was a relatively new friend of Kerry's. Vicky had just split from her husband and so Kerry thought it might be nice for her to come along to the party. This was all I knew about her at the time.

On the day of the party we were sitting in the games room having a drink and a good time when Kerry arrived with Vicky. As pleased as I was that they had both come, I looked at Vicky and just thought, 'Oh dear!' All at once I felt the urge to go over and talk to her. I had a bad feeling about something although at this stage I didn't know why. As the girls went off to get themselves a drink at the bar on the other side of the room I couldn't take my eyes off Vicky. I didn't mean to be rude and stare but try as I might I couldn't let her out of my sight. As I looked at her this elderly lady came through to me and told me that she was Vicky's grandmother. She was giving me a warning. As I say, I didn't know Vicky and I didn't want to scare her, but the message I was getting in my head was so strong and clear that I knew this feeling would not go away until I had passed it on to her.

I had to speak to her somehow so I went over to her and acted casually, as if I was just having a normal chat with her.

After a minute or two I looked at her and without really knowing what I was saying began reading for her. The messages and images I was receiving were coming through fast.

'Have you just moved house?' I asked her.

'Yes,' Vicky replied.

'Is it a stone house?'

'Yes,' she said, now looking a bit bewildered by my interrogation.

'Is the house a three-storey house?' I continued. Vicky nodded her head.

'Who is Sam?' I asked.

Vicky's puzzled look changed to one of fear. 'My little boy!' she said.

'And Amy?'

'My little girl.' Vicky now looked worried. I hadn't meant to scare her but I just felt that I had to check to see if this message was for her, and now that I knew it was I realized I had to pass it on. I asked Vicky if Sam slept on the top floor. She said that he did. I described his bedroom in detail with his single bed positioned in the corner of the room. I could see a picture of the room in my mind's eye. It was as though I was staring at a photograph of it. There was a lot of blue in the room but as I studied this image in my head I suddenly saw flames. Sam's bed was on fire! Vicky's gran was showing me this so that I could warn Vicky.

'There's going to be a fire Vicky,' I said. 'But you can stop it if you listen to me.' Vicky stared at me in disbelief but nodded all the same. 'There is a plug in his room to which a television and his computer game are connected.' Vicky nodded. 'From this plug is a wire. Lift the carpet up and you'll find it. Follow the wire and it will lead you into a loft cupboard. There are a lot of cases in this cupboard and if you take them out you will see that this wire is connected to a socket, which is in the loft's floorboards. Around the plug is newspaper, which has been put there to keep the socket in place. This socket is going to blow and burn Vicky, mark my words. You must get it checked out before you let Sam sleep there again.' Vicky nodded silently. She looked horrified and pale. I knew I had scared her, but to be honest I had intended to because I knew that I had to warn her. Who knows what would happen if I kept my mouth shut.

Now what I hadn't known at the time was that the night before the party Vicky had been talking to a friend called Jane on the telephone. Jane was asking if Vicky felt happy in her new home and Vicky had said yes. But then she added, 'You know Jane, I just don't know what I'd do if there was a fire here.' I think that Vicky had been concerned about the fact that Sam's room was at the top of the house and she was worried about how she would get to him if a fire started.

It just so happened that Vicky's father was an electrician. When she told him about my warning and about her own fears she asked him if he would mind popping over and checking out the wiring for her. I think he was slightly sceptical. 'You shouldn't listen to all that,' he said to her, but sensing her concern he agreed to give the wiring a once over and came over the next day.

Once in Sam's room he followed my instructions. He lifted up the carpet, found the wire I was talking about which led him to the loft cupboard. Under the pile of suitcases he found the socket in the floorboards just as I had described. Around the socket was a lot of crumpled newspaper, which had been stuffed into the socket to keep it in place. He couldn't believe his eyes, not least because the wire leading to the socket was live. 'There is no doubt about it,' he told people later. 'That was a fire just waiting to start; it was simply a matter of days before it started,' he said. 'Had Rita not said anything to Vicky then that whole room would have caught fire in seconds. She saved Sam's life,' he said.

Not all warnings come to me in the form of audible messages from the spirit world. Sometimes the warnings I receive come to me in dreams or through flashes in my mind's eye. Over the years I have been woken in the night by many bad dreams, only for them to occur days later. I have seen planes fall from the sky, been woken by the gut feeling that someone I know is going to pass away, and predicted the terrorist bombing of a shopping centre. What is deeply frustrating about these dreams and premonitions is that more often than not I am powerless to do anything about them. I am never quite sure why I am being given these images – perhaps my spirit guide sends them to prepare me for the worst or to let me know that I will soon be reading for one of these people affected by the events that I have seen.

Sometimes I find that I am sent warnings that have to do with my own life. A few years ago Mo and I went to our holiday home in Skegness for a break. We had been out shopping that day and I had bought myself a beautiful green dressing gown. Now as a rule I never wear green. My grandmother always used to say, 'black follows green Rita, it's not the colour for you'.

What she meant by that wisdom is that if you wear green be prepared for bad luck, because green is unlucky, and so it will be that you'll soon be dressed for mourning. So all my life I have avoided green, but when I saw this dressing gown hanging in the shop window I knew I had to have it. It was made of the softest material, was embroidered and was a pale hue of green. 'It's so pale I can get away with that,' I thought. So with my wallet in hand I marched into the shop and took possession of my wonderful new robe.

The next morning I was standing in our caravan making our breakfast. Mo had gone outside to move the car and I was standing in front of the cooking range cooking some bacon. Suddenly there was this terrible back draught from the pan, and the sleeve of the dressing gown nearest the pan caught fire. Within seconds the fire had spread all over me – I was on fire. I felt the heat of the flames melt the dressing gown on to my skin. I was screaming for Mo. I couldn't put the flames out. My hair was now on fire, so I shook my head from side to side in a vain attempt to put the flames out. Suddenly it stopped. I opened my eyes and there I was standing in front of the cooking range. There was no fire; there hadn't been. Sure enough I had burnt the bacon a little but my dressing gown was fine, it wasn't even singed. Mo walked through the door and looked at me. 'That bacon smells good,' he said.

'Mo, didn't you hear me scream?' I asked, completely bewildered.

'No,' he said. 'I didn't hear a thing. Why?'

There is no doubt in my mind that what I saw was a warning. It was sent to me either by my spirit guide or by my grandmother. I didn't wear that green dressing gown again on holiday. In fact I never wear it in the house. I keep it by the pool and put it on only when I've been for a swim and I make sure I stay pretty close to the water when I've got it on!

The problem with premonitions is it's sometimes not that easy to understand what they mean. Often the images and warnings I receive from my spirit guides do not make immediate sense to me. The images are extremely vivid but I am not always sure how to interpret them. When I was still living at Ash House I woke up just before seven in the morning. Mo was still fast asleep but I decided to get up and so crept quietly out of the bedroom so that I wouldn't wake him. I went to the kitchen and was running the tap to fill the kettle when I suddenly saw Mo dressed in his overalls through the kitchen window. He was being dragged across the garden and into a bush. I couldn't believe what I was seeing! There was no way in the time it had taken for me to leave the bedroom and enter the kitchen that Mo could have got up, got dressed and be in the garden. What was even more odd about the vision I had just seen was that from our kitchen window at Ash House you couldn't see the garden through the window. The kitchen window faced on to the out-buildings. When I looked again I could not see Mo or the garden – I was facing a view of the stable wall. I walked to the bedroom and put my head round the door and there was Mo sleeping soundly. 'I must be still asleep,' I thought to myself.

A couple of months after we moved to Mill Lane Farm my granddaughter Denise brought her horses Domino and Storm over because it had been decided that we should keep them in the field in front of the house. They had only been with us a couple of days and they were beginning to settle in. One afternoon someone had been firing shots on the land below our house. Domino, who is an old gypsy cast horse, was obviously frightened and had somehow escaped from the field and found his way on to the patio. Mo went outside and managed to grab him and was steering him back into the field with a leading rein. Just as he managed to shut the field gate another shot was fired and a terrified Domino bucked and galloped off across the field. I was sitting inside at the time when suddenly I saw Mo on the ground being dragged along by the horse. His hand must have got stuck in the rein and he couldn't let go. Domino was heading down the driveway towards the hedge. I honestly thought he was going to be trampled to death. Eventually Mo managed to free himself from the rein. As I ran from the house he lay on the ground obviously shaken and in a lot of pain. I looked down on him in his overalls – it was only then that I realized that I had been warned of this accident long before it had happened.

Another problem with futurizing is that the messages I am asked to relay to people seem so strange, so improbable, so far-fetched that is difficult to know how or whether to pass the message on or not. Sometimes I will tell a person about something that is going to happen in their future and they just stare at me in total disbelief! I know what they are thinking. 'She was right about my past and pretty accurate about my present, but what she has said about my future is just plain ridiculous.'

I once told a girl I read for that the man she worked for would shortly ask her to marry him. So far I had been right in the reading about everything to do with her life and relationships but when I told her this she just burst out laughing. 'Oh don't be absurd,' she said. 'I'm not even having a relationship with him. Not only is he my boss but he is thirty years older than I am! You must be confused.'

'I promise you it's the truth,' I said. 'Mark my words.' And so I went on to tell her when this would happen. I described the place in which he would ask her. I gave her his name, told her the model of the car he drove, correctly told her that he had once lived abroad, and said, 'He has been married before but it was very brief.'

'Well you're right about all that,' she said. 'But he has never been married. I know that for a fact.' A month later she called me out of the blue. 'Rita, you won't believe what I am about to tell you,' she said. She didn't have to continue because I already knew. Her boss had proposed and it was in a Greek restaurant, just like I had described. I had said that there would be live music, that they would be in a basement and that they would have driven there in his dark blue BMW. They had been talking about work, just as I said, when he came out with it just like that. He admitted that he had been in love with her for a while and confessed that when he was very young he had been married but his wife had left him for another man.

'Well, what did you say?' I asked.

'I was so shocked I couldn't speak,' she said. 'Not because of the proposal because you had told me that, but because what you said was true!'

Premonitions and warnings can come to me at anytime and at any place, which can be difficult for me. I don't have to be con-ducting a reading from home to start hearing or seeing warnings from the spirit world. It's something of a standing joke in these parts that I am able to come into a pub for a drink and tell people what's wrong with their car. 'You want to get that seen to, your brakes are faulty!' I'll say. Or, 'You must get that white van of yours in for an MOT tomorrow.' I'm usually pretty spot on but given the fact that I know nothing about cars and can't even drive I sometimes even amuse myself. The fact is that when spirits want to warn you of something they go out of their way to make me pass that message on. It doesn't matter where I am or what I'm doing, once the message comes through they'll not stop going on at me until I've said my bit. Often I find it easier just to stay at home because frankly I find it awkward approaching a stranger and passing a message or warning on to them, especially if it's sinister. I don't like alarming people or unnerving them.

One night, a couple of years ago now, Mo and I decided to go out for dinner. Mo had planned to take me to a local pub called Bateman's Mill, where they do the most wonderful food, and so he had booked a table for the two of us. Bateman's Mill is one of my favourite places so initially when he told me I was thrilled. However, just before we were about to set off in the car for dinner I suddenly had a change of heart.

'Let's not go there tonight,' I said to him as he opened the car door.

'Why ever not?' he asked. 'I thought you liked it.'

'Oh I do,' I said. 'But tonight I think we should go to The Red Lion, instead.'

'Are you sure?' he asked.

'I couldn't be more sure,' I replied. I had no idea why I had changed my mind but all I did know is that we had to go to The Red Lion that night. It was as though I was being drawn there.

When we arrived at The Red Lion Mo found us a table and a waitress came over to give us our menus. As soon as I set eyes on her I knew why we had come. It was to give her a message. As she poured our drinks and set the table for us I couldn't keep my eyes off her. I knew that she recognized me and no doubt scared of me, she avoided eye contact. I tried to get the voice out of my head but it was no use. 'Oh God!' I thought to myself. 'Here we go again!' One of the problems with my job is that sometimes you just can't switch off, call it a day, unwind and relax. Once the spirits come, and they want to pass a message on, well that's it! You're stuck with them until you have done what they want. That's all very well and good but I don't want to go round scaring people. I find it difficult, as you can imagine, simply turning round to perfect strangers and saying, 'I've got a message for you.'

I didn't want to scare this poor girl but I knew I had to speak to her because I felt that something very bad was about to happen to her that night. So when she came back to the table to take our orders I looked at this girl, who can't have been more than nineteen, and said, 'Is your name Susan?'

'Yes,' she said looking nervously from side to side. I knew she was wondering how I knew her name – she wasn't wearing a name badge and she hadn't seen me at The Red Lion before.

'Can you sit down for a sec, love,' I said calmly. Susan sat down and stared at the table.

'How are you getting home tonight?' I asked.

'I was going to walk,' she said. looking at me with her great big eyes.

I knew at once she was a Pisces so decided to tread carefully. 'Can't you get a lift?' I asked. 'Or a taxi?'

'No,' she said. 'I don't finish my shift until 10 p.m. and my car's in the garage. That's how I normally get to and from work, but tonight I thought I'd walk. I don't live far. Ten minutes away if that.'

Now Susan may have only lived ten minutes away from The Red Lion but the route to her house took her from the main road down a dark country lane, with fields on either side.

In my mind I was getting a strong warning. I could see this lane and the fields. This image kept flashing through my head. I described the lane to her. 'Yes, that's it,' she said.

'Susan, are there gypsies living in the fields around you?' I asked.

'I don't know if they're gypsies,' Susan replied. 'But a whole load of caravans arrived in the fields yesterday.'

In my mind the flashes came together. I didn't want to scare her so I said nothing. I could see the caravans and a bonfire. And I could see Susan walking home in her coat. I saw the gypsies and saw two of them, two men, walk away from the fire and walk towards the road, then I saw them attack her and rape her. I saw her struggle but it was no good. One of them was holding her down. She didn't stand a chance. 'You cannot let this happen,' I kept hearing in my head. 'You must stop it. Don't let her walk home tonight.'

'Susan,' I said, taking her hand. 'You're not walking home tonight. If I have to take you myself, you'll not go home alone down that road, lovey.' Susan's large eyes widened and she went quite pale. I knew that I had scared her but what could I do – the images were so vivid, the voice in my head was so strong, that I couldn't ignore the spirit guide.

Susan went back to work and brought us our food. Mo and I stayed there until 10 p.m. waiting for her shift to end. We drove her home, turning from the main road into the dark country lane. It was exactly as I had seen it in my vision. As we got to the end of the lane and turned the corner into her driveway we saw the caravans, we saw the fire and the gypsies. I said nothing. Susan got out of the car outside her door and we saw her into the house. When we turned the car round and drove back into the lane we caught sight of two men, slightly worse for drink, standing near the edge of the road. 'You know, I'm glad we drove that girl home,' said Mo. 'I don't like the look of those men at all.'

'Nor me,' I replied. I didn't like the look of them standing there either, and I hadn't liked the look of them when I had seen them in my head at The Red Lion.

8. *From Beyond the Grave*

One of the most rewarding aspects of my work is when I know that I have passed on a message from the spirit world that helped someone and made a difference to their life. I am not just talking about helping to solve crimes and mysteries. Sometimes it is the tiniest message, the one that means little to me, that has the most dramatic impact on the life of the person left behind.

Telling a young woman whose father passed away the year before that he travelled from the spirit world, came to her wedding and walked with her down the aisle – and being able to prove it to her through the details I relay – is just as rewarding as helping to solve a crime.

Spirits really do watch over and protect us as I hope that I have shown in this book. They are always with us, taking care of us and looking out for us, and you don't need to go to a medium to have this proved to you.

Spirits try and communicate with us through our daily lives. What we need to do is learn how to read the signs. Many people write to me with stories of how they believe their loved one's spirit has come to them. As we have seen earlier, sometimes when spirits come to us they let us know by playing with electrical equipment such as turning a radio on or off, or by causing interference with the television reception, or fiddling with the lighting. I don't think the spirit is trying to be mischievous or naughty, although sometimes I think they can be brazen in their attempts to get our attention, but a spiritual presence seems to affect electrical frequencies. At other times people notice more natural phenomena – birds, butterflies and cats, seemingly wild animals which suddenly become tame around you – which seem to symbolize the presence of their loved one. I believe it is their spirit coming to you. People often tell me how a particular flower – for no reason – has suddenly bloomed and flourished in their garden since their loved one passed over. Usually it is a plant that they loved very much in this life. All these are messages and symbols that come to us from our loved ones on the other side. These are their calling cards, if you like.

Spirits don't just come to us through nature and electricity. They come to us in our thoughts and in our dreams too. When we dream of our loved one at night it is usually because they have come to us while we are sleeping and been with us. The dream is a sign that they were there, particularly if the dream wasn't something to do with the past. You may dream that they have been with you and when you wake you are left feeling warm and happy. In these instances your loved one's spirit has been with you, so you shouldn't be sad when you think it was just a dream. The likelihood is it wasn't.

Spirits come to us in our thoughts by placing ideas in our heads. We have all had those times when we are just about to pick up the telephone and call someone only for it to ring and it to be the person we were calling. 'How odd!' we say. 'I was about to call you – you must be psychic!' They may not be psychic but your spirit may have made them think of you at that precise moment. Some people call it coincidence, sometimes it is simply just that, but at other times it is due to spiritual intervention.

We can feel someone staring at us even though our back is turned to them. The reason we know we are being stared at, even though we cannot see it, is because our spirits are making us feel it. In *Soul Mates* I discussed how spirits bring people together in unusual ways. I described how suddenly you meet someone you haven't seen for thirty years and you fall in love. Or how you can literally bump into a stranger and end up spending the rest of your lives together. Spirits intervene and interfere in our lives like this because they want us to fulfil our destinies, because some things are fated to happen to us and they know that they can help us. Whether they are reuniting us with people we have lost or finding things for us or helping us at work, spirits are always on hand for us throughout the day. They are always at hand beyond the grave.

Spirits can also stop things from happening to us by influencing our minds and actions. I read for a mother who told me the following story. One morning she went to the chemist by car to pick something up. Now she was a good mother and protective of her baby son. She was used to taking him everywhere with her no matter how short the journey, carrying him in a papoose on her back. That morning as she was opening the back of the car to get him out of his baby seat she heard a voice telling her to leave him in the car. She would never normally have done this but as though she were on autopilot she opened the back window a little, locked the car and crossed the road to the chemist. As she was coming back to the car she crossed the road again but a speeding car shot from around the corner and knocked her on to the ground on her back. Had she taken her child with her she would have killed him falling in the way that she did, but thanks to the intervention of her spirit guide she only broke her leg.

In much the same way, spirits can put things in our paths that can help us, or indeed as this next story shows, can help save our lives. This is the story of a wonderful man called Jimmy, who is in his mid thirties and lives in London. About fourteen years ago Jimmy's life, to quote him, 'fell apart and lost all meaning'. His parents suddenly divorced, he was living and working on his own, running his own picture-framing business, and although close to his sister he felt alone. Over the years his depression got so bad that on many occasions he felt like taking his own life. He wanted to escape this 'bitter world' as he put it. 'I felt like I was dead and just going through the motions of life,' he said afterwards.

A couple of years ago Jimmy felt once and for all that he had had enough. So he sat down and planned a day when he was going to take his life. He decided that he would take an overdose of pills, go to sleep and never wake up again. Spiritual intervention, however, was to get in the way of his plans.

Having planned to spend his last weekend with his sister he arrived at her house on Friday evening. They had a pleasant weekend together, talking, seeing people and catching up. On Saturday night Jimmy found that he was unable to sleep, so at about 4 a.m. he got up and went downstairs to watch television. Jimmy's sister must have heard him because she joined him downstairs and they began to have a deep talk. He told her how unhappy he was and all his problems, and she just listened. She then said to him that she had been reading my book *From One World to Another*. She said that she was convinced that reading this book could help with his problems and so she lent it to him. Jimmy didn't want to read the book but not wanting to offend her, took it anyway and promised to read it when he got back home.

That Monday night when he was back in his flat Jimmy started to prepare for his suicide. He counted out a dose of pills, got some alcohol and began to write notes. This wasn't a cry for help. Jimmy was intent on taking his life. As he was sitting there composing a note to his family, smoking a cigarette, for some reason he has never been able to explain he felt an urge to pick up the book. He opened it up and read the contents page, the preface and on and on. When he got to Chapter Five he got up, took the note from the table and burnt it. 'It was obvious to me what I had to do,' he said. 'I felt so ashamed with myself I cried like a baby.' He said that as he read the book he felt stronger and less alone, he found direction, a path.

I am convinced that it was Jimmy's guardian angel that made him feel compelled to pick up the book, and it was the book – the stories of other people's courage and the afterlife – which gave him the will and the strength to go on. Frankly, I am pleased, because he is a lovely man with a life worth living. I would rather that one man like Jimmy reads my book and finds it helpful than wish for thousands of book sales!

As I showed in *Soul Mates*, spirits will often go out of their way to reunite us with our loved ones. Spirits cannot bear to see us unhappy and they hate to think of us missing someone who is here on earth plane, so they will always do their best to get us back together, because they see this as an unnecessary grief. When I first met my hairdresser Helen I knew at once there was a sadness in her and her husband Mark's lives. Their spirit guides were asking me to help them, so one day out of the blue I asked her if I could read for her and Mark. Here she continues the story in her own words.

I had been doing Rita's hair for a couple of months when one day she asked if she could read for Mark and me. I was taken aback by this. Rita didn't know us at all well at that stage but of course curiosity and all that, I agreed. Mark and I had both been married before and recently Mark had been having a very difficult time with his ex-wife. Without wanting to go into too much detail Mark had given up the right to see his kids when they divorced and this was causing him the most awful amount of pain. I suppose that in some way I thought that Rita might be able to help him through this difficult time.

When we went to see her for the reading Rita mentioned Mark's kids straightaway. She told us that she was talking to someone called Tom, who she said was Mark's grandfather. Mark's grandfather was called Tom so we were impressed by this. Rita said that Tom was telling her to tell Mark that the kids were OK. Although Rita knew that Mark and I had both been married before I had never mentioned the problems that Mark had been having with access to his kids.

Tom was telling Rita that he watched over them. They were all right and Mark should know that he would see them again soon –

one day they would be reunited. She told us that there were three children and Tom was saying that Mark's youngest had a birthmark on her tummy. Well that completely blew us away because she does, but she was born after Tom had died, so it proved to me that he was watching over them.

Mark's ex-wife had moved house in the autumn of 2000 but she hadn't told us where she was going. We had tried hard to get hold of them but with no luck. We simply didn't have a clue where they were. 'You'll find them,' Rita said. 'They're not far from here.'

Rita proceeded to tell us that the kids were in Matlock, in Nottingham. She said she could see a stone-built terraced house, that she could see a number 3 and a 5 on the door. We were slightly surprised by the idea of a terraced house. Mark's ex-wife had married a man with three kids of his own, so we assumed that they would be living in a much larger house. But Rita was adamant. 'It's a three-storey stone terrace,' she said. 'I know it is there because I can see three children riding on bikes in a circle and your youngest has got a brand-new bike.'

Now I was quite nervous about following up Rita's information. I thought it could be awkward if we just showed up. What if Rita was wrong? But Mark was keen to give it a go and Rita was sure it was the right thing to do. 'Go,' she said. 'It will do you all good to see each other.'

So one weekend we got in the car and headed for Matlock. We drove around for quite a bit searching for stone-terraced houses but had no luck. We were just about to give up when we turned into a street of three-storey stone terraced houses. We drove down slowly when all of a sudden there it was – Mark's ex-wife's car. We drove past it to the end of the street so that we could turn round in the cul-

de-sac when Mark saw his kids. All three were on their bicycles riding around in a circle round the cul-de-sac. We stopped the car and got out and the kids came running to Mark. The youngest ran right up to him, flung her arms round him and said excitedly, 'Look at my new bike Daddy!' It had been given to her that day as a birthday present. Mark nearly fainted!

If you have been close to someone in your life and they pass over they will make sure that they never leave you. At times of upmost grief we tend to cry out to the person who has passed over and ask them, 'How could you leave me alone?' Although the person that we loved here on earth is no longer physically with us you shouldn't imagine that they have abandoned us. They are constantly by our side. For this to happen it doesn't have to be someone close to you – in other words your children, parents or spouse – often the person who is watching over you could be an old childhood friend, a mentor or a colleague we have known from work, even someone who has touched our lives very briefly. I find the bond is already there in the cases where a grandparent has died before their grandchild has come into this world. They watch with love and pride in the same way that they would if they were still around. Spirits always want to help us and make our lives better places. They care for our well-being on every level whether it is at work, rest or play as I think this next story demonstrates.

I have been reading for a couple called Robert and Cathy since the beginning of the nineties, and they come to me for readings still, about twice a year. I started reading for them because I once read for Cathy's mother and she recommended that they come and see me. At the time of their first reading Robert, who is a graphic designer, was having problems with his business. He was self-employed and ran his own company. I think that Robert was sceptical when he first came to see me and I got the feeling that he wasn't quite sure why he was there. Anyway I wanted to tell this story because I think it shows how spirits can help us in all aspects of our lives. This is his story told in his own words.

I was pretty sceptical about going for a reading with Rita. I hadn't been to a medium before but Cathy's mother had said that she was amazing so I think I just thought why not. I wasn't sure I believed in all of that but I had nothing to lose. Within ten minutes of our first reading I was completely amazed. Rita said things to us that blew me away. She mentioned the names of the people I knew in spirit, she told me that my grandparents watched over us, everything that she said about our past and present was accurate. I was amazed.

What I think really took me aback that afternoon was when she started to talk to me about my business. I work as a graphic designer and run my own company. For a while in the early nineties we had been having a few serious problems. When Rita started talking to me about the company and what was going wrong I couldn't believe my ears. She was using terminology and words that to be honest only someone in this kind of profession might understand. Knowing Rita as I do now this is always the more amusing because Rita, by her own admission, knows nothing about graphics or business. She still doesn't really know what I do and she always says at the end of each reading that she hasn't got a clue what she has said, that it means nothing to her at all. 'It's not me that says this, you know, it's your spirit guides,' she'll say.

That day Rita said that one of the problems we were having with the company had to do with a certain individual who she named. Cathy and I had had our suspicions about this person all along but hadn't acted on them. Here was Rita sitting in front of me telling me about this man. She told me that he worked for me but that he had been offered a job with our main competitor. For the moment he was sitting pretty in our firm while he passed on our secrets and strategy. She told us that this was why we were having financial problems and had seen a slump in our business. Perhaps I wouldn't have been so convinced had Rita not described our offices so vividly, down to the floor even.

Over the years Rita has talked to me about my work. She has told me what negotiations I am involved in, which staff to take on even though she has never met them, she uses the jargon of the trade and has correctly given me figures from contracts we have had. The influence and help she has given Cathy and me in our work has been astounding. Again when I thank her she'll always say that it's my family in spirit who are helping me. The effect she has had on our lives doesn't just extend to our work. She has helped us in other ways too. Cathy and I have a daughter called Lucy who we both adore. A couple of years ago when Lucy was eight Cathy and I decided that we wanted to go away for the weekend. We were off to a hotel and to test-drive a car, and had planned to take Lucy with us. At the last moment one of our relations stepped in and said that she would love to have Lucy and that she thought it would be nice if we had a break.

The week before our trip we went to see Rita and she said to us, 'What's Lucy doing this weekend?' This was odd because we had never mentioned to Rita that we were going away and we always spent every weekend at home with Lucy. So we told her that she was going to relatives. 'Do they live near a river?'

'No,' I said, 'why?' Rita told us that she was getting a strong feeling about a river. She kept asking us if we were sure. We were positive, we told her.

'I'm sorry,' she said to us, 'I am just getting a bad feeling to do with a river and Lucy.' That Friday we called Rita. 'I'm still getting a bad feeling about the river,' she said.

I told her not to worry because we had decided not to go for the weekend. 'Lucy is staying with us,' I told her.

'Good, because I was worried about her. I could see her in her little pink jacket with hooks, her white tights and her black patent shoes,' she said. 'And I was worried that something bad might happen.'

When I repeated this to Cathy she looked at me in total disbelief and showed me into Lucy's room where on the bed Cathy had laid out Lucy's clothes. Amongst them were a pink toggled jacket, white tights and a brand-new pair of black patent leather shoes, clothes Lucy would have worn had she gone for the weekend. Later that day my relation called to say that there had been a terrible accident on the main road outside her house that afternoon. 'Which road do you mean?' I asked, unsure.

'You know River Road, Robert, the main road!'

I wanted to end this book with a wonderful story that starts off sad but I think you will agree has a beautiful and positive ending. This story shows not only how a spirit helped shed light on the mysterious circumstances of their death, but how they helped bring someone to me for a reading and how the messages that I relayed to this woman during our session helped her make sense of a tragedy and gave her the strength and courage to move on with her life.

This story is about a wonderful woman called Norma who comes from Scotland. After her husband Paul, a member of the merchant navy, passed over she tried hard to get in contact with me. She was desperate for answers about what had happened to Paul and must have written me ten or so letters. Eventually she got hold of me. I am gald she did because I was able to help her. She tells her story here in her own words:

My husband Paul passed over on 12th February 1998. He died at sea. He was in the Merchant Navy. I was a teacher and a sea wife. We were married for twenty years and were deeply in love. We never had children so our world was all about him and me and the love that we shared.

The week that Paul passed over he was at sea and I had gone to spend the half-term break with Carol and Martin, some friends of ours. I returned home that Thursday night and went to bed early. I was woken later that night by a banging on the front door. I had a good mind not to open it at the time but did so nevertheless. There was a man at the door. As soon as I saw him standing there I knew why he had come. He had been sent to tell me that Paul was dead.

From that moment my world collapsed; it just fell apart. I had lost the love of my life. My husband and I were very close. We were everything to each other. The worst thing about my grief was that I never knew what happened to him. Of course there had been reports but they took a long time to come through. Paul had passed over in the waters off Singapore. *A blunt blow to the head, they had said. In other reports they mentioned the fact that Paul had fallen down some steps. I wasn't sure what had killed him. Had it been the blow to the head, the fall, was he alone, had he been pushed? I had no idea. The reports came from all quarters, but none of them conclusively told me how Paul had gone. After a while I gave up searching the reports for answers and my family fielded most of them. By this stage I was too tired to go into any more. I was distraught and I felt that my life was over.*

For my birthday, a year after Paul passed over, Carol and Martin gave me a book. It was called From One World to Another. *It was by a medium called Rita Rogers. By that stage I had read a great many books by mediums but there was something about this book that I found compulsive. I am not sure what it was. I think that I could just identify so much with the people mentioned in the stories, and being Scottish her story about finding the missing soldiers in the Cairngorms appealed to me.*

Soon after I read the book I wrote to Rita. I needed to talk to her because I so needed to know where he was. I must have written ten letters to her. I knew that she was popular but I also knew that I needed to talk to her and find out what had really happened to Paul. I wanted so many answers. Was he a victim of foul play, had he been alive when he fell down the stairs of the ship or had he already gone? I wanted to get to the bottom of the mystery. Eventually I found out that Rita wrote for a magazine and so I wrote to them asking if I might be able to have a reading with her. I didn't honestly think anything would happen but days later I came back to hear a message on my machine. It was from the magazine — they wanted to know if I wanted an appointment. I could not believe it! I was like a Jack Russell tearing round and round. At last I was going to talk to Paul. Finally I would know the truth.

I always call my reading, my reading with Rita and Paul, because that's what it was like. I wasn't just talking to a medium. I was talking to my husband through her. At once she told me that she had a 'lovely man' with her and that he was my husband and my soul mate. 'He is telling me that he was in uniform and at sea,' she said, just like that. She described a large boat, 'like a rig'. 'Was he in the navy?' she asked.

She told me about this lovely man. 'A helpful man whom every-one adored', which was so true of him. She described his smile and his wonderful eyes. Now Paul was the most handsome man. I am not just saying that he was. People would comment on it all the time. I loved Rita for what she said next. 'He could drive the ducks off the water with his eyes, lovey,' she said to me. 'He was a very handsome man, wasn't he?'

She told me that my name had been on his lips when he passed over and that he came to me straightaway. She told me he was there when the man came to break the news to me, but that he had come to me before that. Earlier that night when I was driving home for no reason I suddenly swerved. I couldn't understand it at the time, but now looking back that must have happened around the time of his passing. That is when he came to me.

She then told me what I had waited all this time to hear. 'He is being very persistent about this but he wants you to know that he died of natural causes.' Then she said to me, 'He says, "Who'd have thought it!"' That was the moment when I knew. I believed there and then everything that was being said to me, that I was talking to Paul, that he had passed over from natural causes — because that was his expression. He'd say that line after everything.

Rita told me that Paul had been suffering from severe headaches at the time he went. 'There was nothing you could have done about it,' she said. She told me he had a strong heart, which he did. And that he had gone quickly. She said that it was an embolism of the brain, a bit like a brain haemorrhage. 'He wasn't in pain,' she said. 'It was just one of those things.' 'It was just one of those things,' — another of Paul's favourite expressions. She told me how I had taken him to the station; again this was amazing because I never usually took Paul to the station. 'That's where you were last together.' These statements just kept flooding through, one after the other, and all the time I was crying, though not with pain. I think I was crying because I knew Paul was there. She told me he kept calling me 'his Norma'. That's what he would always say, 'My Norma!'

'He's laughing a lot,' she said. 'He's got a great big laugh and he's telling you not to be sad. He says that he was "too good for this world" and he's laughing.' Paul was always very cheeky and naughty and used to wind me up by saying to me, 'You know Norma, I'm too good for this world!'

This reading gave me the will to go on. Rita and Paul answered all the questions that had bothered me, the things that had kept me up at night, that had stopped me from mourning and from getting on with my life. Until that moment I was a desperate woman, one with no hope who thought she had no future. Hearing how Paul had passed over was a great relief to me, but knowing that he is with me means much, much more. Since that reading I have got on with my life. I have carried on with my teaching, have taken a course and I am about to open a dress exchange in Scotland. Funnily enough the square the shop is on is 'St Paul's Square'.

This year I sent flowers to Rita to mark the anniversary of my reading, of the moment I spoke to Paul again, and it is an anniversary I will always keep.

AFTERWORD

We spend our lives looking for answers, explanations and proof. If we do not have tangible hard evidence of the existence of something then we tend to be suspicious of it or to disbelieve it. By having closed minds we create our own mysteries in many respects. As a medium, I am lucky, because the proof I receive on a daily basis through my readings has convinced me of the existence of an afterlife. Of course, not everyone is lucky enough to have this gift and this knowledge, but by opening our minds and accepting that there is a life after this we can come to understand a great deal, not only about the course of our lives, but also about ourselves.

RITA ROGERS

Learning to Live Again

PAN BOOKS £6.99

A Practical, Spiritual Guide to Coping with Bereavement

Grief is one of the strongest emotions that we face, arising as it does from the deep wells of love, affection and habit that tie us to one another. It is difficult to articulate the painful and often conflicting feelings that emerge from the various natural stages of grieving. But Rita Rogers, with her extraordinary gift for dealing with loss, can shine a light into that darkness, revealing that the people with whom we have shared love and friendship in this life can live on, albeit in another dimension, looking out for us and leading the way.

With compassion and understanding, Rita is our companion throughout the grieving process, reassuring us that even our most destructive and isolating feelings are part of a natural reaction. Addressing particular losses – of young and older children, of siblings, parents, friends, soul mates and those lost by suicide or in tragedies – Rita reaches across the divide of death, bringing the energy, the joy and the memories of those lost lives back into our broken hearts, and helping us all to learn to live again.